PRAISE FOR
DATA-DRIVEN HR

Without doubt human capability (talent, leadership, organization and HR) increasingly delivers value to all stakeholders. This excellent book provides business and HR leaders the information required to improve decision making. Its insights on analytics and AI will be the keys for progress.
Dave Ulrich, Rensis Likert Professor, Ross School of Business, University of Michigan, and Partner, The RBL Group

If anyone was going to publish a book about the impact of the latest technology developments such as AI on the field of HR and people analytics my bets were on Bernard Marr. And you won't be disappointed. The book offers a deep dive into the world of data of every kind, every possible use case, honest overview of technology and important considerations. It has never been more critical to educate ourselves about it.
Maja Luckos, VP, Employee Success, Salesforce

This book propelled me into a world of possibilities for HR leaders in embracing the 'intelligence revolution' to shape people strategies that add value to their organisations and their people. It's enlightened me to the power of AI-enabled HR and how I might use it, and it's made me want to learn more. This is a must-read for all HR leaders.
Linda Sleath, Group HR Director, Topps Tiles

Data-Driven HR strikes a nice balance between exploring emerging trends in people analytics while primarily serving as a practical guide to HR professionals at any stage of their data journey. This second edition seamlessly weaves AI into a narrative that's easy to engage with and is packed full of examples that bring the theories to life.
Mark Ferrie, People Analytics Director, Meta

Data-Driven HR is a terrific overview of the enormous world of people analytics and AI. For people trying to understand this important space, this book shows you the way.
Josh Bersin, Global Industry Analyst and CEO of The Josh Bersin Company

Data, analytics and AI provides ways to elevate HR from its traditional role as a support function to one of a strategic partner creating value for the enterprise, its customers and its employees. There's a well-thumbed copy of the first edition of *Data Driven HR* on my bookshelf, and in this timely update Marr, one of the most knowledgeable people on the topic, explains how data and AI can enable HR to drive better decision making about people, deliver an enhanced service to employees and make HR processes more efficient.
David Green, Managing Partner at Insight222, co-author of *Excellence in People Analytics*, and host of the *Digital HR Leaders* podcast.

Bernard Marr has once again delivered an indispensable guide to harnessing the power of data, analytics, and AI in HR. This updated edition thoroughly captures the latest innovations shaping human resources while still being accessible for HR professionals at any level. Through compelling examples and clear frameworks, Marr demonstrates how to drive business value through evidence-based talent practices. This is a must-read playbook for any HR leader looking to build capabilities in data-driven decision-making.
Professor Max Blumberg, University of Leeds

This is a great guide for HR professionals who are grappling with the transition to becoming data led. It's easy to read, and with real examples and case studies across the employee lifecycle, it's also a pragmatic resource to have in your HR toolkit.
Matthew Mee, Talent Innovation, Vice President, Lightcast

Artificial Intelligence is here, and this is just the beginning. As always, Marr takes a highly complex topic and decodes it in a way that it is understandable for people at all levels – be it 'people for people (HR)' or the more technical proficient experts who want to understand the people aspect of what AI brings to table. As Marr explains with great simplicity it's not all about the technology, but about how we as humans learn to coexist, embed it in our day-to-day work lives and more, answering critical questions and innovatively thinking about the impact it will have on the future of our workforce, acceleration in building the analytics capability and maturity across organisation is a MUST HAVE. *Data-Driven HR* is an excellent build from his previous edition of this title.
Ashish Sinha Korn Ferry Head of People Analytics, AI & Strategy EMEA Practice Leader

AI is transforming the world of work and our personal lives. With a people-centric approach, Bernard Marr demystifies data driven AI enabled HR with context, thought provoking insights and examples of AI at the time this book was written. We all have a role to play when it comes to this rapidly evolving space as the output of AI will be a reflection of our culture and values. Staying on top of leading practices, lessons learned, emerging regulations and standards is critical so we can unlock AI's potential and value add to the business, our customers and employees while minimizing risk. This book sets the foundation so we can do just that.
Terilyn Juarez Monroe

Data-Driven HR is an indispensable resource for career services professionals looking to equip their students with cutting-edge strategies in today's competitive job market. This comprehensive book offers invaluable insights into recruitment and candidate selection, employer branding, pinpointing the most effective recruitment channels, and harnessing AI-enhanced automation to identify and assess the best candidates for businesses. It's a game-changer for career advisers committed to empowering their students with the knowledge and skills needed to excel in the evolving world of talent acquisition and HR.
Amber Wigmore Álvarez, Associate Professor, IE Business School and IE University, Spain

Second Edition

Data-Driven HR

How to use AI, analytics and
data to drive performance

Bernard Marr

First published in Great Britain and the United States in 2018 by Kogan Page Limited
Second edition 2024

2nd Floor, 45 Gee Street	8 W 38th Street, Suite 902	4737/23 Ansari Road
London	New York, NY 10018	Daryaganj
EC1V 3RS	USA	New Delhi 110002
United Kingdom		India

www.koganpage.com

Kogan Page books are printed on paper from sustainable forests.

ISBNs

Hardback	978 1 3986 1458 1
Paperback	978 1 3986 1456 7
Ebook	978 1 3986 1457 4

British Library Cataloguing-in-Publication Data
A CIP record for this book is available from the British Library.

Library of Congress Control Number
2023948898

Typeset by Integra Software Services, Pondicherry
Print production managed by Jellyfish
Printed and bound by CPI Group (UK) Ltd, Croydon, CR0 4YY

To my wife Claire, the heart of our family, and to my children Sophia, James, and Oliver, its soul.

You embody the essence of this book: that at the core of any successful endeavour, even in a world driven by data and technology, are people.

CONTENTS

PART TWO Data-driven and AI-enabled
HR in practice

How data and AI 01
are transforming
HR

We're in the midst of a new industrial revolution – the fourth industrial revolution, driven by an explosion in data, automation, intelligent machines and hyper-connectivity. Like the previous industrial revolutions before it (the most recent being the rise of computerization in the late 20th century), this new wave of transformation will utterly change the way we live. And, of course, the way we work.

The last few years have seen dramatic change for organizations across almost all sectors. No doubt you've seen signs of this in your own job, as the organization begins to take advantage of new technologies. That change is only going to accelerate over the next five to ten years.

And yet, at the heart of our rapidly changing organizations are… people. Companies are nothing without the right people. Even in this technology-driven age, those organizations that are able to attract (and keep) the right people are most likely to succeed now and in the future. As businesses navigate rapid change, this need to attract and nurture talent is arguably *more* important, not less. Now more than ever, people are the central driver of success.

It's therefore vital that human resources (HR) teams put in place the intelligent systems and processes to find, recruit and retain the right people for their organization. Which brings us to the need for data-driven, AI-enabled HR.

HR and the 'intelligence revolution'

I call this fourth industrial revolution the 'intelligence revolution' because that's exactly what it is – a revolution that's creating an increasingly super-intelligent, data-driven world. Artificial intelligence (AI) and the intelligence revolution will transform so much of our everyday lives, just as the rise of computers did in the previous industrial revolution. (Maybe even more so. Sergey Brin, co-founder of Google, has described AI as 'the most significant development in computing in my lifetime.'[1])

Every business – and every function within the business – is going to have to get smarter. This is equally true whether your organization is operating in one of the more obviously contemporary industries, like the tech sector, or a more traditional industry, like manufacturing. And it's true whether you work for a global corporation or a small start-up business.

The good news for HR professionals is that you have more data at your fingertips than ever before. Now, almost everything we do at work can be measured: from employees' day-to-day actions, performance, happiness and wellbeing to wider business operations. This, coupled with advances in analytics – largely driven by AI technologies – means the HR function has the potential to access incredible insights. This is the age of *data-driven, AI-enabled HR* – or as I'll sometimes call it in this book, *intelligent HR*.

Defining intelligent HR

Data-driven, AI-enabled HR is about harnessing this data explosion and new analytics tools to drive performance – within both the HR team itself and the wider organization.

What does this look like in practice?

There are many ways HR teams can make good use of data and AI, but, broadly speaking, they boil down to three main categories:

- Unearthing the insights needed to drive better decision making (by which I mean HR decision making and decision making across the organization).
- Delivering a better HR service to employees (for example, through improved recruitment and onboarding processes, or an enhanced employee wellness offering).
- And making HR processes more efficient (for example, through automation).

This idea of data-driven, AI-enabled HR has gathered enormous pace in the last couple of years as new software tools have emerged to serve the HR function. There's a whole market of off-the-shelf HR analytics tools, for example, that help HR professionals get the most out of data without any knowledge of data science or AI algorithms. These new technologies are making HR more data-driven, agile and responsive, while providing employees with more personalized and engaging experiences.

Ultimately, this business function that has traditionally focused on softer elements like people, culture, learning and development and employee engagement is becoming increasingly driven by data and analytics. That's not to say people aren't still at the centre of everything HR does – of course they are. Rather, data and analytics are providing exciting, innovative ways for HR teams to serve those people.

It's all about adding value

With data-driven, AI-enabled people management, the top priority is always to *add value* to the organization, using all the tools at the HR team's disposal, including data, sensors, analytics and AI. What you want to avoid is technology for technology's sake. Because, yes, you can do some really cool stuff with data and AI, but if it doesn't add value to the organization, what's the point?

Everything you do with data and AI must therefore help the HR function and the wider organization deliver its strategic objectives. Whether you want to address employee turnover issues, build a winning employer brand, boost performance in certain parts of the business or whatever, data and AI can help you achieve your goals and solve your biggest challenges. Sounds grand, doesn't it? But as the examples in this book show, it is absolutely possible. HR teams are already gaining tantalizing benefits by using data and AI in strategic ways to unearth business-critical insights.

Take Google's often-touted approach to people management as an example. Google gives staff free meals, generously paid holiday allowances, access to 'nap pods' for snoozing during the day and space to grow their own fruit and vegetables at work. Now, I'm sure Google's leadership team is full of lovely, generous people, but that's not why they implemented these policies – or, at least, it's not the only reason. These decisions were based on what the data told them would increase employee satisfaction. Google's approach to boosting staff satisfaction thoroughly disrupted the tech world, dramatically changing the way Silicon Valley employers think about employee perks, and now tech companies of all sizes, from the big players to small start-ups, seek to emulate the Google approach. And, while staff turnover is consistently high in the tech world, Google remains one of the most desirable tech brands to work for.

A (brief) word on automation

There's been a lot of talk about the rise of automation and the threat this brings to jobs. From factory line jobs to professions like accounting and architecture, AI technologies like machine learning – where a computer 'learns' from what the data is telling it and adapts its decision making and actions according to what it's learned – mean that more and more tasks can now be automated and completed by machines or algorithms. As we'll see throughout this book, a lot of HR tasks can now be automated. In many cases, machines can perform a task to a much more accurate degree than a human can. Algorithms can predict employee churn better than a human ever could, for instance.

AI and automation will therefore have a major impact on HR over the next five years or so. One Oxford University study looked at the types of jobs that would be affected by automation, and concluded that, by 2035, HR administrative jobs had a 90 per cent chance of being automated.[2] HR officers, managers and directors, however, were much less likely to be replaced by machines.

What does such automation look like? One good example is virtual help-desk agents – chatbots, essentially – that could answer simple employee questions such as 'When is the company closed over the Christmas break?' or 'How much of my annual leave have I used already this year?' AI technology is now so sophisticated that it can respond to natural, spoken language, rather than typed questions, and even detect the underlying sentiment behind the words themselves. Call centres, for example, are using this technology to analyse whether a caller is satisfied, frustrated or angry during the course of their call.

So, it's clear that HR will be affected by automation over the next few years. However, in the context of intelligent HR, this should be seen as a positive development. Automating the simpler, administrative-type tasks frees up HR professionals to focus on more important tasks that align with the company's strategic vision and help deliver performance improvements.

Of course, there's also a wider issue around automation – and that is the impact on jobs elsewhere in the organization. As we'll see in this book, automation doesn't necessarily mean that people will lose their jobs (indeed, more jobs will be created). But it does mean that people's jobs are likely to evolve somewhat, as machines take on more and more tasks. HR will play a critical role in preparing the organization for this change, for example by upskilling and reskilling the workforce, and by building a culture of adaptability and flexibility. But we'll talk more about that later in the book.

How to use this book

My goal in this book is to explore the key ways in which data and AI can drive performance, both in terms of the HR team's own performance and value within the organization, and in terms of how data-driven, AI-enabled HR can help drive performance right across the business. I think of this book as a journey, looking at the developments that have brought us to this point and identifying a path forward for HR professionals.

With this in mind, Part One lines up the building blocks of intelligent HR, including creating a data strategy, and identifying the different data and analytics options. We'll also look at some of the potential pitfalls and concerns around using data and AI, including privacy issues, bias and the need for transparency. As we'll see in Chapter 4, the way a company uses data and AI, and how that is communicated to staff, has a big impact on how people react. Ill-considered, poorly communicated or discriminatory uses of data and AI erode trust, and can be extremely harmful to morale. Thankfully, there are plenty of ways HR teams can mitigate these potential issues and gain employee buy-in, and we'll look at some of those in Chapter 4.

Part Two looks at intelligent HR in practice, and how data and AI can drive operational improvements and better decision making across all the core HR functions: people analytics, recruitment, onboarding, performance monitoring and management, training and development, and employee safety and wellbeing. I cannot stress enough how all of these functions are already being transformed by data and analytics. In these chapters, I'm not making wild predictions about potential future developments. The future is already here. The challenge for HR teams is to ensure they're continually adding maximum value to the organization through data and AI – while maintaining a people-centric approach.

Finally, in Part Three we'll put what we've learned into action, exploring how to identify (and prioritize) data and AI use cases for your own organization, how to build the right skills and culture for data-driven, AI-enabled success and what to consider in terms of technology and infrastructure.

And throughout the book you'll find plenty of real-world examples that showcase how companies across all sectors are using data and AI in incredible ways. I hope these examples inspire you to tackle this exciting new world head-on.

At the end of each chapter, I'll summarize the critical learning points. Even if you only manage to skim over certain parts of the book, these key takeaways will give you the absolutely must-have info in one simple list.

Key takeaways

Here's what we've learned in this chapter:

- Almost everything we do at work can now be measured, from employees' day-to-day actions, performance and wellbeing, to wider business operations. This explosion in data is all part of the fourth industrial revolution – the 'intelligence revolution', which is being driven by data, AI, automation and connectivity.

- This explosion in data, coupled with AI-driven advances in analytics, mean that HR teams can extract insights that improve the performance of people within the company (including its HR team), and contribute to the organization's overall success.

- With data-driven, AI-enabled HR, the top priority is to *add value* to the organization through technology – while, at the same time, maintaining a people-centric approach.

- There are many ways HR teams can make good use of data and AI, but, in their most basic sense, they boil down to three main categories: unearthing insights that drive better decision making across the organization; delivering an enhanced HR service to employees; and making HR processes more efficient.

Now, let's start our journey into data-driven, AI-enabled HR by exploring how we got to this point. In Chapter 2 I look at the evolution of intelligent HR, and how the explosion in data and analytics technologies, including AI and the Internet of Things (IoT), is making HR more intelligent than ever before.

Notes

1 J Vincent. Google's Sergey Brin warns of the threat from AI in today's 'technology renaissance', The Verge, 28 April. www.theverge.com/2018/4/28/17295064/google-ai-threat-sergey-brin-founders-letter-technology-renaissance (archived at https://perma.cc/3JH5-9XQH)

2 S Shah. Will AI augment or replace HR? HR Magazine, 1 December 2016. www.hrmagazine.co.uk/article-details/will-ai-augment-or-replace-hr (archived at https://perma.cc/QS42-V76V)

PART ONE
Laying the groundwork for data-driven, AI-enabled HR

Organizations have seen enormous transformation in recent years, driven by new technologies and automation. And the HR function is not immune from this change. Far from it – the way in which organizations attract, retain and nurture talent is becoming increasingly shaped by new data and artificial intelligence tools.

In this first part of the book we'll explore how data and AI are changing the HR function, and how this transformation came about. We'll also explore the foundations of 'intelligent HR', including the types of data available today, the different analytics options, the challenges that surround data and AI, and how to use data and AI strategically in your organization.

How data and   02
AI have come to
revolutionize HR

Within the wider context of work, human resources is a relatively new function. Yet, in its short – roughly century-long – history HR has evolved significantly. And that change has been particularly pronounced over the last 20 years, driven by an explosion in data and the evolution of AI technologies. Today, technology plays a vital role in the work of HR professionals. But how did we get to this point?

In this chapter, we take a quick tour through the history of HR and explore how data and AI (as well as other technologies) have found their way into the HR function.

The emergence of HR and its early evolution

We can trace the history of HR back to the late 19th century, when the concept of 'personnel management' first emerged.

The Industrial Revolution took employment from 'personal' to 'personnel'

Coming in the wake of the Industrial Revolution, the late 19th century was a time of huge technological and societal change. Processes that had traditionally been done manually were now mechanized, thereby changing the work that humans did. In general, work shifted from agricultural labour and small-scale manufacturing towards work in large factories. And this, in turn, changed the nature of employment. Someone who had previously worked with their family, or for a local, small-scale business might now be one of potentially hundreds of employees in a large company – with no direct relationship with the owner of that company. In other words, the closely connected relationship between employer and employee was, by and large, a thing of the past. And this prompted a need for business owners to hire people to manage the employee relationship – hence, personnel management. In these early days of personnel management, the focus was largely on administrative tasks such as hiring and payroll, as opposed to looking after people. Working conditions were often not great (to put it mildly), and employee concerns often went unheard – prompting a period of unrest and clashes between employees and employers. In America, this was known as the 'Progressive Era', a period of social activism and reform aimed at defeating (among other things), corruption, poverty and the exploitation of labour.

Moving into the 20th century

Amidst this societal change, in the early 20th century the focus of HR shifted more to managing employee relations and grievances, as well as making sure the company complied with labour laws. It's fair to say the work of HR professionals during this time was largely reactive, rather than proactive – dealing with employee concerns, for example, or negotiating with employees over working conditions.

This began to change in the 1960s and 1970s, as HR started to focus more on strategic planning and organizational development, with HR professionals working to align HR practices with the organization's wider goals.

But even during this period, as HR began to noticeably evolve, it was still highly reactive. Within organizations, HR was often seen as the 'corporate police' – making sure employers and employees complied with new legislation on discrimination and harassment, and dealing with the fallout when rules were broken. Ask the average manager in the 1970s what HR did and their answer would likely be along those lines: policing people's words and actions. You know, compliance stuff.

By the 1980s and 1990s the 'personnel' departments of old had evolved into the 'human resources' function that we recognize today – one that emphasizes the importance of employee development, performance management and talent management. This is really when HR professionals began to work more closely with managers and executives to ensure that the organization had the right people in the right positions to achieve its goals.

And this evolution was matched by a technological revolution. To some extent, HR has always been rich in data – employee records and so on – but there was no widespread effort to analyse and harness that data. But in the

1990s, HR departments began to adopt HR information systems (HRIS), which allowed for the automation of routine HR tasks such as employee record keeping and benefits administration. These systems also provided HR professionals with access to data that could be used to monitor and analyse HR trends and performance.

It was this digital revolution of the late 20th century that paved the way for a new era of data-driven HR.

The turn of the 21st century and the beginnings of data-driven HR

The early 2000s saw the emergence of talent management systems, which allowed organizations to better track and manage employee performance and development. These systems provided HR professionals with more sophisticated data analysis tools, allowing them to make more informed decisions about talent management. This empowered HR professionals to work in a much more strategic and forward-thinking capacity.

Of course, hiring, compliance and dealing with employee grievances remain a core part of the HR function, but from this point onwards HR is recognized as having a critical impact on an organization's success. People are a huge part of what distinguishes a business from its competitors. Talent is a key differentiator. And the HR function over the last 20–30 years has evolved to help organizations get the most out of their talent.

HR in the 21st century: The rise of people analytics

Building on the emerging data-driven approach of the early 2000s, in recent years there has been an even greater shift towards *people analytics*, or using data to gain insights into the workforce and to inform HR decision making. This includes analysing data on employee engagement, turnover, productivity and diversity and inclusion – and then using insights from that data to inform decisions and action.

The role of AI in HR

Increasingly, this data-driven approach is becoming more proactive and predictive. Rather than simply looking at what *has been*, with AI tools HR professionals can predict future trends and identify potential areas of risk.

AI seems like a very recent addition to the HR function, but in fact the history of AI in HR can be traced back to the early 2000s. At that time, the focus was on automating routine HR tasks such as resume screening and candidate sourcing using rule-based systems. It wasn't until the mid-2010s that AI began to be used for more sophisticated HR tasks such as predicting employee turnover, identifying high-potential employees and identifying the best candidates for specific roles. In one example, IBM used AI to predict – with 95 per cent accuracy – which employees were most at risk of leaving their job.[1] The predictive attrition program saved the company almost $300 million.

From the mid-2010s onwards, AI was also being used to automate certain HR functions. For example, AI-powered chatbots were introduced to improve the candidate and employee experience by providing immediate responses to frequently asked questions.

The explosion in data

Without data, these advancements in AI would not be possible. Data is what allows an AI system to identify patterns, spot trends and make predictions about the future. Lucky, then, that people generate so much data! Almost everything in a business context generates data, from an employee sending an email to the sensors on production line machinery.

What's more, employers can now collect types of data that simply weren't available before. This includes things like capturing employees on closed-circuit television (CCTV), scanning social media data for employee sentiment, analysing the content of emails and even monitoring where employees are using the data from sensors in corporate phones. I'm not saying it's necessary for employers to gather data on every little thing – indeed, data for data's sake is something we want to avoid – just that it is now possible to gather more data, and more *varied* types of data. We're no longer talking only about neatly structured data in databases and spreadsheets, but also unstructured data such as text and video content. There's also a wealth of HR-specific data, such as recruitment data, career progression data, training data, absenteeism figures, productivity data, personal development reviews, competency profiles and staff satisfaction data.

Bottom line, businesses have more data to mine for insights than ever before. In the past, people-related data mostly went unused or, if it was used, it was put into charts and tables for something like a corporate performance pack. It's the advancement of AI that has allowed HR teams to truly harness this data and extract value from it.

Amidst this explosion of data and AI, HR has become the function that supports the strategic use of people-related data – gathering that data, analysing it and sharing the insights with decision makers across the organization. I guess you could say the name 'people analytics' is slightly misleading, since it is much more about improving strategic decision making and performance in order to drive the business forward – but since that data is generated by the people working within the business, 'people analytics' it is! By the mid-2010s professionals were being recruited into specific people analytics roles within HR functions. And in 2020, LinkedIn's global talent trends 2020 report listed people analytics as one of the most important trends in human resources.[2] People analytics had officially arrived.

The changing technology landscape – and its impact on HR

It's clear that data and AI have advanced enormously in the last decade. In the last few years, technology has advanced at a pace that even I – an expert in future tech trends – find eye-opening. So let's spend a brief while exploring the wider technology context and the major tech trends that will increasingly impact the HR function.

Future internet technologies like the metaverse and blockchain

We're entering the third evolution of the internet, often referred to as Web3 or Web 3.0. Blockchain is one of the core features of this future internet, since blockchain is the technology that underpins things like cryptocurrency and non-fungible tokens (NFTs).

In its most basic sense, blockchain is a way of storing data. Like a database, but built for the future internet and with much better security than your average computer system. Just one of the ways blockchain can improve HR processes is in validating resumes, in a system where people's credentials live 'on the blockchain', and can be validated by previous employers, universities and even government departments (validating the candidate's identity, for instance).

So, blockchain is one future internet technology to watch. Another feature of the future internet – and potentially one that has wider-reaching implications for HR – is that the online world will become much more *immersive*. And this brings us to the metaverse…

The emerging concept of the metaverse is geared around persistent, shared virtual worlds – immersive digital spaces where we can play, socialize, shop, learn, exercise and even work. Mark Zuckerberg once described the metaverse as being *inside* the internet, rather than just looking at it through a screen, and I think that's a great description. Largely this will be enabled by immersive metaverse technologies like virtual reality (VR).

The Fortnite universe gives us a glimpse of how the metaverse will impact life. In Fortnite, users aren't just there to game; they buy outfits and accessories for their digital selves, hang out with friends and even attend virtual gigs (by superstars like Ariana Grande). So, the metaverse enables people to spend more time in virtual environments, and those environments will be more immersive, realistic and engaging than today's online experiences.

Crucially, in this new evolution of the internet, the lines between the real world and the virtual world become even more blurred than they are today. And this will influence the world of work. Instead of logging on to a Zoom meeting, for instance, remote employees will be able to put on their VR headset and join a virtual meeting room, with realistic avatars of their colleagues. Employees will be able to work and train in the metaverse, in virtual co-working spaces or digital replicas of real-world offices. And there will be new ways for colleagues to collaborate on projects virtually in real time. Consider, for example, that Meta and Microsoft are teaming up to put Microsoft tools, including Teams and Windows, on the new Oculus VR headset.[3]

The metaverse will even change the way we hire and onboard employees. For example, Samsung hosted a virtual recruitment fair to attract candidates,[4] and PwC has created its own metaverse space, Virtual Park, to give candidates an insight into what it's like to work for the company.[5]

We'll touch on the metaverse and blockchain throughout the book, but if you want a really deep dive on the topic, you might be interested in my book, *The Future Internet: How the metaverse, Web 3.0, and blockchain will transform business and society.*

The importance of AI

The metaverse and blockchain are both enabled by AI, which again puts AI (and, in turn, data) at the centre of the digital revolution. Note that I typically use 'AI' as a catch-all description, but what we're often talking about is *machine learning* – the specific subset of artificial intelligence focused on creating machines (computers, software, etc.) that are capable of learning from data in a way that's similar to the human brain.

AI capabilities are advancing fast, and AI is increasingly able to take on the work that was traditionally thought of as human. For example, we have generative language AI models that can write text that's pretty much indistinguishable from that of a human writer. The GPT tool by OpenAI can create anything that has a language structure – which means it can answer questions, write essays, summarize long texts, translate languages, take memos and even create computer code. The technology is advancing to such an extent that it can create computer code based on natural language prompts. In other words, GPT can build apps and software for users who don't have a background in software design. Even just a few years ago this wasn't possible.

AI is evolving at an incredible rate, then. And, as such, it is inextricably linked with other technology trends. Trends like the Internet of Things, the ever-increasing network of smart devices that are connected to the internet – from watches and phones to fridges and coffee machines. Such devices are constantly gathering and transmitting data, further fuelling the growth in data and AI. And trends like chatbots and voice interfaces (think Alexa and Siri), which are able to communicate so well because of AI. And trends like robots and cobots (collaborative robots), which are becoming more intelligent, learning to perform tasks without human intervention or work seamlessly alongside humans, thanks to AI.

Naturally, such widespread technological change is impacting how people do their jobs and how HR serves the organization. We'll talk about that throughout the book. For now, let's also acknowledge that the very nature of work itself – and our attitude to work – is changing.

The changing nature of work

As the HR function has become more data-driven, it has also had to grapple with some widespread changes in the world of work.

The employee experience

These changes were drastically accelerated by the Covid-19 pandemic, which fuelled the adoption of technology and remote working in many sectors, and caused many people to re-evaluate what they want from work. On top of that, more young people are entering the workforce. And these younger generations expect, more so than older generations, to connect with their employer in a meaningful way.

So, while the human resources functions of the past might have focused more on grievances and compliance, they are now very much focused on creating an employee experience that drives business performance and boosts the acquisition and retention of talent. Things like an awesome onboarding experience, flexible working arrangements, generous benefits (beyond salary), a strong organizational purpose, and so on.

Changing organizational structures

The way organizations are structured is changing too. The traditional, rigid and hierarchical organizational structures of old are giving way to flatter, more agile structures that allow the business to quickly reorganize teams and respond to change. This move towards flatter organizational structures is also, in part, a response to the proliferation of freelance workers.

More and more people are engaged in gig working, whether it's on a full-time basis or as a side hustle. The rise of gig working, coupled with a wider move towards remote working, has massively opened up the labour market. An organization's next hire could be based on the other side of the world, for instance. They could be a freelancer who has to integrate and work with an existing team. This creates both opportunities and challenges for companies. In a global labour market where candidates are no longer limited to local employers, organizations must prioritize the employee experience and demonstrate a strong purpose if they want to attract and retain the best talent. As we'll see throughout this book, data and AI can add huge value to this process of creating an enriching employee experience – from recruitment and onboarding to employee wellbeing.

The impact of automation

There is also rising automation to consider, particularly when it comes to striking the right balance between human workers and intelligent robots. We now have increasingly capable robots and artificial intelligence systems – chatbots, for example – that can take on tasks previously done by humans. This leaves the HR function with some key questions, such as how do we find the balance between intelligent machines and human intelligence? What roles should be given over to machines? And which roles are best suited to humans? There's no doubt that automation will affect every industry, and much of the responsibility for preparing organizations – and people – for this change will fall to HR. If you're interested in reading more about these (and other) business trends, you might like to check out my book, *Business Trends in Practice: The 25+ trends that are redefining organizations.*

New skills for a new era of work

The changing nature of work and rapid acceleration of technology will impact the kinds of skills that employers need. The majority of children entering school today will do jobs that don't yet exist. (Sound far-fetched? Consider that we didn't have social media managers, podcast producers, influencers and blockchain developers a generation ago.) And for many people already in the workforce, their jobs will evolve or even become obsolete.

In a world in which more and more jobs (and parts of jobs) are given over to intelligent machines, the essential skills that organizations require will evolve. Naturally, organizations will need more digital skills, but distinctly human skills will also become more valuable – the kinds of things that machines can't do as well as us. Skills like complex decision making, emotional intelligence and empathy, creativity, teamwork and adaptability. We'll talk more about essential skills later in the book but – as you might have guessed – I also have a book on the subject. It's called *Future Skills: The 20 skills and competencies everyone needs to succeed in a digital world.*

So what lies ahead for data-driven HR?

Overall, the use of data in HR has evolved from simple record keeping to sophisticated people analytics that inform key HR decisions. As technology continues to advance, it is likely that data and AI will play an even more important role in HR in the years to come.

Challenges and opportunities

The increasing use of data and AI brings challenges. I'll talk more about this in Chapter 5, but one of the biggest challenges will be ensuring that AI is used ethically and fairly. There's a risk that AI-powered systems could reinforce biases or discriminate against certain groups (there are many examples of this already happening, often because the underlying data itself is skewed for or against certain groups). To address this, HR professionals must be trained to use AI responsibly and ensure that their algorithms are transparent and unbiased. And that the underlying data isn't biased.

There will also need to be transparency around exactly what data organizations gather from their employees, and why. Consent is key. But going above and beyond consent, we also want employees to fully buy into the use of data and analytics because they understand how it will benefit their job and the organization as a whole. Careful communication is needed.

Despite the challenges that lie ahead, the use of AI in HR is expected to continue to grow in the coming years. This is a good thing. With the increasing availability of data and advances in machine learning, AI has the potential to revolutionize HR by providing insights into employee behaviour, predicting workforce trends and improving the overall employee experience.

Data, AI and major HR trends

Before we close out this chapter, let's briefly explore some significant future trends in HR. Because it's clear that data and AI have an important role to play in these trends...

One HR trend that we've already touched on is the hybrid working environment that employees will increasingly enjoy. The role of technology in general is pretty obvious here, since it will allow remote employees to collaborate with colleagues in new ways. But while flexible working brings many benefits to employees, it can sometimes have a negative impact on engagement, connection and satisfaction. Data and AI can help HR functions monitor these factors and ensure that employees remain engaged even as the physical working environment changes.

Employee wellness is a perennial trend in HR, but more attention is being paid to mental health. Among other things, data and AI can help organizations monitor how employees feel about their mental health, assess the effectiveness of employee assistance programmes, and design an employee experience that supports good mental health.

Another trend is addressing the talent exodus. In the wake of the pandemic, many people left their jobs, or searched for jobs that offered them a better work–life balance (or, simply, more meaning). In certain sectors – technology and IT being a great example – there are more job openings than there are candidates, so holding on to talent is a primary objective. Data and AI can be used to improve the hiring and onboarding process, and identify the benefits that resonate most with people. And that's just for starters. As we've already seen in this chapter, there are predictive AI systems that can identify the employees most at risk of quitting – which is incredibly valuable information to a proactive HR team.

AI analytics can also add real value to diversity, equity and inclusion (DEI) programmes – not just when it comes to assessing DEI in the workplace, but also finding a way forward. For example, analytics can help business leaders understand employees' thoughts on belonging, intersectionality and bias in the organization.

And since upskilling the workforce will be a major task in this age of rapid digital transformation, it makes sense that learning management is another major trend in HR. AI-enhanced learning systems allow employees to learn online at their own pace and enjoy a more personalized learning experience.

These trends give us just a small taste of what AI and data can bring to HR practices in future. But don't worry, we'll talk more about specific HR practices in Part Two of the book.

Key takeaways

Let's finish with a quick summary of what we've learned in this chapter:

- In its relatively short history, HR has undergone a major evolution – from the admin-focused approach of old, to a more strategic approach where the work of HR aligns with organizational goals.

- Particularly in the last 10 years or so, HR has adopted more of a *people analytics* approach, using data and AI to inform decision making and drive business performance.

- The last few years have seen major digital transformation – not just in terms of data and AI, but also in terms of future internet technologies like blockchain and VR. In the future internet, as the metaverse evolves, we will spend more time in virtual environments, and this will impact the world of work.

- At the same time, there are other major shifts taking place in the world of work. From hybrid working and changing organizational structures to the need for a stellar employee experience, HR functions are grappling with widespread change.

- Data and AI will play an increasingly important role in HR, helping HR professionals navigate the challenges that come with rapid transformation, and leverage the many opportunities that will arise from new ways of working.

No doubt about it: this is an exciting – and challenging – time to be an HR professional. I hope this chapter has given you a sense of how we've arrived at this point in time, where people analytics plays a central role in HR. Now let's explore these AI tools in a little more detail. Turn the page and discover some of the revolutionary data, analytics and AI tools available to HR.

Notes

1 E Rosenbaum. IBM artificial intelligence can predict with 95% accuracy which workers are about to quit their jobs, CNBC, 3 April 2019. www.cnbc.com/2019/04/03/ibm-ai-can-predict-with-95-percent-accuracy-which-mployees-will-quit.html (archived at https://perma.cc/DSK9-VVFC)

2 LinkedIn. Data-driven insights into the changing world of work, LinkedIn, May 2023. business.linkedin.com/talent-solutions/global-talent-trends (archived at https://perma.cc/FBF4-372U)

3 A Kidwai. Meta and Microsoft form an unlikely partnership on workplace VR, HR Brew; 19 October 2022. www.hr-brew.com/stories/2022/10/19/meta-and-microsoft-form-an-unlikely-partnership-on-workplace-vr (archived at https://perma.cc/AQ3H-ABCA)

4 L Handley. Looking for a job? You might get hired via the metaverse, experts say, CNBC, 30 November 2021. www.cnbc.com/2021/11/30/looking-for-a-job-you-might-get-hired-via-the-metaverse-experts-say.html (archived at https://perma.cc/8TXT-2JCE)

5 PwC. PwC's Virtual Park, PwC, 2023. www.pwc.co.uk/careers/early-careers/ourevents/virtual-park.html (archived at https://perma.cc/J9UE-P525)

The data, analytics and AI tools available to HR

03

These days, most HR functions are rich in data. But that's not the same as being rich in *insights*. For that, you need to be able to turn data into valuable insights that answer your biggest people-related questions, and help you solve problems, drive performance and boost the employee experience. This is where analytics comes into play.

Analytics is the process of collecting, processing and reporting data to generate insights. In most cases, we use analytics tools and algorithms to do this. By analysing data with algorithms and analytics tools, you can extract critical insights that will help the HR function perform its role to the fullest.

The amazing capabilities of analytics and AI tools (and how to use them in HR)

Traditionally, data would have been queried using tools like Excel and structured query language (SQL – used to interrogate databases). These methods of analysis have served businesses fine for decades and still form the foundation of many essential business analytics, like analysing revenue. When you're dealing with neat, structured data in spreadsheets and databases, these methods work great.

However, the amount of data that businesses have access to these days increasingly doesn't conform to this traditional notion of data – i.e. that it's numerical and lives in a database or spreadsheet. Much of the data businesses have access to today is in the form of text, video, voice recordings and so on. These sorts of data are more difficult to work with, and as such new analytical methods have arisen to cope with this. Bottom line, we can now use AI-based analytics to do so much more than traditional analytics tools.

A quick overview of AI

AI is a term I use throughout this book as a useful catch-all description. But the term 'AI' loosely groups together specific technologies and methods – the most common being *machine learning, deep learning* and *generative adversarial networks.*

AI is best thought of as an aspiration – we aspire to build intelligent machines that are capable of learning for themselves, just as naturally intelligent creatures such as humans and animals can. This ultimate aspiration of *generalized AI* – AI that is capable of adapting to pretty much any task that a human can do – is way beyond our current capabilities. Instead, today's applications of AI – certainly in a business context – fall under the category of *specialized AI*, which basically means AI tools that are designed to become very good at one task (or group of tasks), constantly learning to improve as they go. And this brings us to machine learning…

Machine learning – the current cutting edge in AI

Machine learning uses techniques that have been around since at least the 1960s to build algorithms that are capable of getting more and more accurate, as they are given more information. In other words, they are capable of learning from data. And the more data you give a machine learning system, the more accurate it becomes. There's been a huge increase in machine learning over the last 10 or so years, largely because there has also been a huge increase in data availability.

But how does an algorithm 'learn?' Well, just like humans, they do it through training and then putting what they've learned to use, assessing the results they achieve and modifying their behaviour accordingly until they work out how to get better results.

Take image recognition, for example. If we have an image and want to know whether it represents a cat, in a very simplified machine learning model we could ask whether it has a tail, whether it has whiskers, whether it has four legs, whether it is covered in fur… and so on. Finally, informed by the decisions it has made already, it attempts to tackle the question 'Is this a picture of a cat?' If the algorithm decides that the answer to all of the initial questions is yes, then it might report to us that there's a high probability that the image contains a cat. If that's all it did, then in our very simple use case it might be quite effective, but we still couldn't say it was 'learning'. If we were to show it the same picture over and over, we would keep getting the same answer, regardless of whether it was right or wrong.

So, machine learning algorithms include a feedback loop, and a system of 'weighting'. Say it looks at a picture of a human, but they are on all fours, and therefore mistakenly answers 'yes' to the question 'Does it have four legs?' It goes on to mistakenly identify the image as a cat. Realizing, thanks to the feedback loop, that it has got this one wrong, it can examine each step of the process and work out where it was most likely to have made a mistake. Through this process – repeated thousands or millions of times – it is able to 'learn' which questions are the best indicators of the correct answer – and adjust its answers (or predictions) in order to take this into account. This explains why we can consider the algorithm to be 'learning'.

Deep learning and neural networks

Think of deep learning as another, more advanced, form of machine learning. As with other forms of machine learning, the principle involves mimicking elements of the human cognitive process. Specifically, deep learning involves the construction of *artificial neural networks* (ANNs) – decision-making frameworks similar to the natural neural networks in the human brain. Due to their size, which is often vast, the ANNs used in deep learning are often called *deep neural networks*.

Deep learning is best used when the problems you are trying to solve are very complex and involve a large amount of unstructured data – for example, understanding and extracting meaning from human speech or images.

Generative adversarial networks

Generative adversarial networks (GANs) are an even more recent development in the world of machine learning, which essentially work by pitting two neural networks against each other, forcing them to learn to work with increasing efficiency in order to outsmart the other one. Essentially, one network, known as the generative network, is given the task of creating a set of data that mimics the rules of a predetermined training set. A piece of data is then taken from either the training set or the newly created set, and presented to the other network, which is known as the discriminator. That network then has to determine whether the piece of data comes from the training set, or the newly created set. If it gets it right, it wins the round. If it gets it wrong, then that round goes to the generative network. Both networks 'learn' from the process, and go on to become even more 'creative' in their attempts to thwart the other. It's a machine-off, basically.

What are GANs used for? They're widely used in the creation of 'deepfakes' – fake (but highly realistic) photographs and videos. They're also used to create AI art, music and writing. In another example, a GAN system created by tech company NVIDIA was able to recreate the Pac-Man game from scratch. After being fed visual data of the game being played, the GAN system managed to generate the entire code for a game of Pac-Man that can be played by humans![1]

Now that we have a basic grounding in AI, let's delve into the specific types of analytics.

The types of analytics available to HR

Before we get into the analytics tools themselves, let me start with a quick word of warning: it's very easy to get caught up in all of the exciting opportunities that analytics offers. This is truer now than ever before, as thousands of vendors are taking advantage of the vast appetite from businesses for anything labelled 'AI'. You'll no doubt see lots of organizations doing very cool things with analytics, but what works for one business may not work for yours. The challenge in using data and AI to great effect is deciding which approach will work best for you, without losing sight of your goals.

Having said that, things are moving so quickly with AI that it's safe to assume that new and improved ways of doing just about anything will emerge even as you're working on your initial use cases. So, while you don't want to get distracted by the 'new and shiny' toys on offer, you do want to keep an open mind about new ways of doing things.

With that out of the way, let's get to the analytics themselves. Because advanced analytics, including all of the machine learning techniques described above, can be used to extract insights in some very exciting ways. Here, we'll take a look at the most applicable methods for HR.

Image and video analytics

These analytic processes are used to extract insight and meaning from any kind of image – still or moving – including photographs and video footage. Machine learning has proven itself to be awesome at this process – providing it's given enough training data and powerful enough computers to crunch through it. Image and video analytics might also include analysing metadata, such as Global Positioning System (GPS) tags on photographs or timestamps on CCTV footage. These give extra insights that wouldn't be available simply from looking at the data by itself.

In the case of video analytics, this gives us the added capability of measuring and analysing behaviour over time. Which is why Tesla's Elon Musk has said that he believes self-driving cars will eventually operate on video data alone,[2] rather than using other sensing technologies like LIDAR. This means they will operate in much the same way as a human driver does, mainly relying on what they see in order to navigate.

In a business context, image analytics has a large number of potential uses, including facial recognition for security purposes, and recognizing products in pictures shared on social media. Video analytics are proving useful in a safety context – for example, to detect when employees aren't wearing the appropriate safety wear or following safety protocols – or simply to understand how employees behave when they're on site.

Text analytics

This is the process of extracting meaning from large quantities of text data. Most businesses have huge amounts of text data – emails, company documents, customer records, websites, press coverage, blogs, social media posts, etc. Thanks to text analytics, this data can now be mined for insights.

The most common text analytics methods include:

- **Categorization** – which involves applying structure to text so that it can be classified by factors such as subject, content, relevance, whether it is fiction or non-fiction, and so on.
- **Text clustering** – which involves grouping text into topics or categories to make filtering easier, in the same way that search engines do.
- **Summarization** – which involves pulling key or relevant points from the document and automatically creating summaries, perhaps personalized for certain people.
- **Sentiment assessment or analytics** – which involves extracting opinion or sentiment from text and categorizing it. (More on this coming up.)

Text analytics is especially helpful for understanding more about your employees. For example, text can be mined for patterns such as an increase or decrease in positive feedback from customers, and this may help to identify customer service representatives who are performing well and those who may need extra support to improve in their role. I know one organization that uses text analytics tools to scan and analyse the content of emails sent by their staff as well as their social media posts. This allows them to accurately understand the levels of staff engagement, meaning they no longer need to carry out traditional (and expensive) staff surveys, and they no longer have to wait to assess staff engagement on an annual basis.

Sentiment analysis

Sentiment isn't only found in text – it can be extracted from video and audio data too, or any other form of data that can be used by someone to express an opinion! Here, the aim is to extract subjective opinions and feelings, in order to determine the attitude of an individual or group towards a particular topic, concept or idea. Sentiment analytics is regularly carried out across social media to understand our reaction to marketing campaigns or new products and services. It's also used by governments and opposition politicians to assess the popularity of policies.

As mentioned, sentiment analysis is very useful when you want to be able to understand stakeholder opinion, be it from customers or employees. Generally, sentiment analysis looks at feelings and opinions as expressed by groups of people, rather than individuals, so it doesn't have to rely on the ability to collect and store personal data. That said, it can also be used to identify individual voices – for example, employees who are amazing advocates for your brand online.

Sentiment analysis seeks to understand the meaning in data beyond what is directly expressed – so by analysing choice of words, context and metadata it's possible to understand, for example, what emotional state the creator was in, even if they don't specifically say 'I'm feeling happy' or 'I'm feeling frustrated.' It can include monitoring and analysing body language in image and video data, for example, or stress levels in voice data (great for analysing customer service calls).

Sentiment analysis is also very useful when you want to understand the attitude of an individual or group regarding a particular topic (such as proposed changes to the company's incentive scheme, for instance) or overall context (wider company culture, for example), and whether that attitude is positive, negative or neutral. In this way, sentiment analysis helps us get at the real truth behind communication. And, in this age of constant digital connectivity and our increasing desire to share our thoughts and feelings about all sorts of things – including companies – online, sentiment analysis has become mainstream.

Voice and speech analytics

This is the process of extracting information from audio recordings of conversations or message logs. This can include analysing the topics and actual words and phrases that are used, as well as the emotional content (sentiment) of the conversation.

Voice and speech analytics is commonly used in customer service settings. For example, it can be used to identify recurring issues in customer complaints or persistent technical problems that occur frequently. Obviously, you can also use this type of analytics to assess the quality of customer service that your representatives are providing, identifying star players whose performance can then be highlighted to others as an example, or poor performers who may benefit from additional training.

You could also use voice analytics to help identify recurring themes around employee satisfaction, or, in the case of a call centre, employee performance. Voice analytics can also help you identify when your employees are getting frustrated or angry. By analysing the pitch and intonations of conversations taking place in your call centre, you can gauge the emotional state and performance of workers.

Analytics as an alternative to some traditional HR tools

I'm not a big fan of those big annual employee surveys. They're expensive. Employees don't find them particularly engaging. And the big danger is people might just tell you what they think you want to hear.

The wide range of analytics tools on offer now can be used to give better and more accurate insights for HR teams. You can, for example, collect data from internal comms systems and social media and then analyse that data using text analytics and sentiment analysis to understand employee sentiment. You can also gain a much deeper understanding of your corporate culture.

Say, for example, you believe that your corporate culture is efficient but fun. You may think that your business operates like a family, with a strong focus on excellent customer service, and those are values that have been driven home to employees. Your orientation for new recruits draws their attention to those values and the corporate culture that you believe exists. But what happens after six months – are those employees embodying those values or is something else calling the shots?

You could ask your new employee or you could conduct annual surveys, but the quickest way to get to the truth is to assess what your employees are *saying* and *doing* as part of their everyday work. That's your culture, after all. If you believe you're driven by high-quality customer service and yet no one answers the phone after 4.45pm, chances are that culture is not quite as real as you'd like it to be.

New analytics approaches can even replace traditional methods of assessing performance. Most companies assess employee performance annually, but, in this world of data, once a year just isn't enough. In order to be effective, performance should be assessed on a regular and less formal basis, and modern data collection and analytics allows this.

Today, we have many innovative ways of collecting and analysing performance. In one innovative example, wearable technology company Humanyze (formerly Sociometric Solutions) has created electronic employee badges that capture information from conversations as they go about their day, including the length of the conversation, the tone of voice involved, how often people interrupt, how well they show empathy and so on. Data from the badges can be analysed in a number of ways, including text analytics, sentiment analysis and voice analytics, and then used to predict which teams are likely to be more successful, which employees are more productive and creative, and which show signs of being great leaders.[3] One of Humanyze's clients, a major bank, noticed that its top-performing employees at call centres were those who took breaks together. Based on this knowledge, they instituted group break policies and performance improved 23 per cent. (Read more about monitoring and managing performance in Chapter 9.)

Tapping into no-code and AI-as-a-service tools

If you've read this far and are interested in putting some of these ideas into practice, but haven't a clue how to build your own machine learning and deep learning algorithms, you're in luck. Because these days, businesses big and small can access AI through a vast number of tools and applications that are available as cloud services. These are often known as *no-code* solutions or *AI-as-a-service*. In fact, AI may already be available in some of your existing cloud-based HR apps. If your people-related data exists in the cloud, you can often just 'plug' it into existing tools and switch on AI capabilities.

What's more, since the GPT tool that we mentioned in Chapter 2 can create computer code based on natural human language instructions, several companies are now creating solutions that harness this potential. So it's likely that, in the near future, it'll be easy for people with zero experience of computer programming to create their own bespoke software applications. No doubt about it, we're seeing the 'democratization of AI' happening before our eyes.

Many of the off-the-shelf analytics tools will also include a data visualization component that helps you communicate the insights you've uncovered. This is important because data-driven HR is about turning people-relevant data into insights and actions that add value to the business. In order to do this successfully, you need to ensure it's easy for the various decision makers, whomever they may be, to extract insights from the data. The easier it is to understand the data and pull out key insights, the easier it is for people both within the HR team and beyond to make decisions and act on that data. This is why data communication and data visualization have become such big topics in recent years.

As mentioned, many commercial analytics platforms will come with their own built-in visualization tools. But there are also inexpensive data visualization tools like Tableau and Qlik available as a service. You can make data look very attractive with impressive visuals, but I think that using a combination of visuals and (short) narrative is much more powerful than using just visuals. For instance, a graph may be a good way of showing employee churn trends over time, but a simple narrative alongside it can pull out the key messages and put that information into context – explaining what might be behind those trends and why there was a spike in churn in late 2022, for example.

ChatGPT as an example of no-code AI in action

I've mentioned the GPT deep learning language model a couple of times already. Now it's time to meet ChatGPT, an AI-based chatbot system that uses GPT's natural language processing (NLP) technology to generate conversations. Launched in late 2022, ChatGPT enables users to ask questions or tell a story, and the bot will respond with relevant, natural-sounding answers and topics. The interface is designed to simulate a human conversation. As such, ChatGPT is capable of explaining, remembering what was said earlier in the conversation, elaborating on ideas when asked, and even apologizing when it gets things wrong.

ChatGPT can be used for a variety of business applications, but for the HR function some of the most enticing uses include:

Recruitment

ChatGPT can automate repetitive tasks in the recruitment process, like screening resumes and scheduling interviews. ChatGPT can also assist in candidate engagement by providing real-time support and answering frequently asked questions about the company and the application process. Plus, HR professionals can use ChatGPT to identify potential candidates who may be a good fit for the organization based on their skills, experience and education.

Employee onboarding

HR teams can set up ChatGPT to provide real-time support and guidance to new hires – including answering common questions about company policies, procedures and benefits, and providing guidance on completing required paperwork. ChatGPT can also help to automate administrative tasks, such as scheduling orientation sessions or sending reminders to new hires about required training.

Training

ChatGPT can provide employees with instant access to training materials and answer questions about workshops and programmes. HR professionals can also automate administrative tasks with ChatGPT, including scheduling training sessions or providing reminders to employees about upcoming events. ChatGPT can even create personalized training plans for employees based on their specific needs and skill sets.

Performance management

ChatGPT can assist in the performance management process by providing managers with guidance on conducting performance evaluations and answering employee questions about performance metrics or feedback. Meanwhile, HR professionals can get real-time insights on employee performance, and they can set up alerts that go to the human resources team as well as to individual managers.

HR chatbots

ChatGPT can be used to develop conversational chatbots for HR departments to improve the overall employee experience. Through chatbots powered by

AI, employees can get instant support for common HR-related questions about things like benefits, vacation policies or payroll.

Employee engagement

ChatGPT can be a useful tool for improving employee engagement by providing workers with real-time support, personalized assistance and instant access to information and resources. It can assist in answering questions about company policies, culture, procedures and benefits, as well as provide guidance on completing various forms and requests.

Compliance

Finally, HR professionals can also use ChatGPT to ensure that their HR policies and practices are consistent, accurate, and compliant with local and national regulations – so they avoid legal or reputational risks that may result from noncompliance.

ChatGPT can also assist in providing employees with up-to-date information on compliance-related matters like employment laws, payroll and tax regulations, and health and safety protocols. The model can also help HR departments track and monitor employee compliance with HR policies, such as attendance, leave requests and work hours.

Bottom line, ChatGPT can be a powerful tool for HR professionals, helping to automate repetitive tasks, provide real-time support to employees and enhance the overall employee experience. Automating these types of tasks can free up HR professionals to focus on more strategic activities.

Getting started with ChatGPT

At the time of writing, ChatGPT is in beta and has already attracted millions of users. If you want to have a go at using the tool, you can. Simply go to chat.openai.com and click 'Sign Up' to set up your account. Once you've created your account, ChatGPT will provide examples of what you can do with the tool, and help you through the process of running your first queries. For now, it's free to use, but it will probably be monetized in future.

A quick word on combining analytics

Often, to get the most out of data-driven HR you won't be able to rely on one analytics tool alone – rather, you'll need to combine different types of analytics. For example, corporate culture analytics may tell you that your culture is moving away from the values you've prioritized, but you may need text and sentiment analysis to tell you why that is. The idea behind combining analytics is to base your decision making and HR operations not just on what one set of analysis is telling you. Combining information from more than one source and using different analytic approaches allows you to verify insights from more than one angle.

All the approaches I've outlined in this chapter show only some of the analytic possibilities available to HR teams today. Just a few years ago, much of this wasn't possible; we couldn't do sentiment analysis on text, for example. Analytics in particular has made such huge leaps that no one knows for sure what's going to be possible in 10 or even five years' time. Therefore, an important part of data-driven HR is staying open to new opportunities that data and analytics may provide further down the road.

Tapping into other data-driven and AI-enabled tech

Before we move on, I want to briefly pause and look at other data-driven and AI-enabled technologies that will prove useful to HR teams – specifically, blockchain and the metaverse. I briefly mentioned both in Chapter 2, but let's explore them in a little more detail to see how these technologies relate to HR.

The potential uses of blockchain in HR

Blockchain first came about as the technical backbone of Bitcoin, but has since evolved into many other uses. Blockchains are essentially a (relatively new) way of storing data online, built around two core features: encryption and distributed computing. *Encryption* means that the data stored on a blockchain can only be accessed by people who have permission to do so, with the use of a special 'key'. And *distributed computing* means that the data is stored across many, many computers or servers, not on one central-ized server. This means no one (other than the person who owns the data) can access or alter the data without permission.

Another thing that makes blockchain unique is the way in which block-chains are structured – basically, as blocks of data chained together, hence the name. Each 'block' is linked to the previous block, thus forming a chain of information. Each block also contains a timestamp to record when the information in that block was created or edited. And, of course, each block is encrypted. As for the information contained within the block, it could be anything: a record of a transaction, a record of ownership rights, personnel information or any other record of information.

Because users can only access and edit the block they 'own' through a private cryptography key, blockchain is very secure. Which is why blockchain is commonly used to help secure and streamline transactions, especially cryptocurrency trading. Such transactions may also involve *smart contracts* – contracts that execute automatically when agreed-on conditions are met. In the future, smart contracts and blockchain could streamline any processes that are heavily reliant on transactions and contracts.

But blockchain is also finding interesting uses beyond transactions. Some governments, including South Korea, are exploring the use of blockchain to manage government records, including digital credentials such as driving licences.[4]

In HR, blockchain uses may include:

- **Verification of credentials.** Blockchain can be used to securely store and verify employee credentials, such as education and employment history. This can help streamline the hiring process and reduce the risk of fraudulent resumes.

- **Payroll and compensation.** Blockchain can be used to automate payroll management and ensure that employee compensation is distributed fairly and transparently.

- **Benefits administration.** Blockchain can be used to securely store and manage employee benefits information, such as health insurance and retirement plans. This can help reduce administrative costs and reduce errors.

- **Performance management.** Blockchain can be used to track and verify employee performance metrics, such as sales numbers or customer satisfaction scores.

- **Employee engagement.** Blockchain can be used to create decentralized, employee-driven platforms for communication and collaboration. This can help to foster a sense of community and engagement among employees, and enable them to contribute to company goals in a more meaningful way.

HR and the metaverse

The concept of the metaverse has existed for a while. In the *Matrix* movies, where humans are locked into a shared virtual world created by machines, that's essentially a (disturbing) depiction of a metaverse. The same with

Ready Player One (a book and film in which people take refuge from our dystopian future world in a massive online role-playing game and virtual society, complete with its own currency). So it's not a new concept invented by Mark Zuckerberg, despite Facebook's clever rebrand to Meta. The metaverse is a concept that society has been building towards for a while – ever since the emergence of the internet, social media, virtual reality and early attempts at creating shared digital environments, like Second Life (the online 3D environment where users engage in an alternative life and assume an alter ego). The metaverse will, in essence, be the next generation of the internet.

The concept of the metaverse is still evolving, but based on Mark Zuckerberg's vision of an internet that you're *inside of*, rather than just looking at, it makes sense that more of our everyday lives will take place inside these shared metaverse worlds. And that includes work.

Which means HR teams must get ready for the metaverse. Some of the ways in which HR could harness the metaverse include:

- **Virtual recruitment.** The metaverse could provide a platform for virtual recruitment, allowing employers to interact with potential candidates in a virtual environment. This could save time and money by reducing the need for physical meetings and travel.

- **Virtual training.** The metaverse could also be used for virtual training, providing employees with a more immersive and interactive learning experience. This could be particularly useful for remote workers.

- **Virtual collaboration.** The metaverse could provide a platform for virtual collaboration, allowing teams to work together in a virtual environment. This could be particularly useful for remote teams, who may struggle with communication and collaboration in a purely digital environment.

- **Virtual meetings.** The metaverse could also provide a platform for virtual meetings, allowing teams to interact with each other in a more natural and immersive way than straight-up video conferencing. This could help to reduce the fatigue and disengagement that can come with long video calls (farewell, Zoom fatigue).

- **Virtual workspaces.** The metaverse could provide a virtual workspace for employees, allowing them to work from anywhere in the world in a fully immersive and customizable environment. This could help to reduce the cost and environmental impact of physical offices, and provide greater flexibility for employees.

Both blockchain and the metaverse are enabled by AI, which in turn means they're reliant on data. So let's turn to the magic ingredient that makes all this possible.

The secret sauce: Data, data and more data

If you're going to use AI and analytics, you need data. Let's explore the data sources available to HR teams, including some of the newer types of data available.

A quick primer on the different types of data

Before we jump in, it's important to remember that no one type of data is inherently better that any other kind. Using data successfully is about finding the data that works best for you and your use cases, and that's likely to be very different to what's best for another use case, or a different business. With so much data available these days, the trick is to hone in on the exact, specific data that holds the most value for you.

The more data, and the greater variety you have, the fuller the picture that you can draw – and the more accurate your analytics will be. In my experience it's often a combination of structured and unstructured, internal and external data that provides the most valuable insights. (Don't worry, we'll define these types of data next.) For example, you may well need to mix some structured, internal data (such as ratings from employee micro-surveys) with some structured external data (data from job portals, perhaps), as well as some unstructured internal data (transcripts from employee interviews, for instance) and unstructured external data (like social media data). Often, it's by combining data that we find the most valuable insights.

Now let's properly define those types of data.

Structured data

Structured data is any data or information that's located in a fixed field within a defined record or file, usually in databases or spreadsheets. Essentially, it is data that is organized in a predetermined way, usually in rows and columns. As such, structured data doesn't really require smart AI algorithms; rather, it's based on simple 'if this, then that' logic.

The average business has the potential to tap into a vast amount of structured data, including employee data, customer data, performance data, sales data, number of website visits and any kind of machinery data points.

Structured data is, for now, the most commonly used type of data in business – yet it represents just 20 per cent of all the data available in the world. The remaining 80 per cent of data out there is unstructured (which we'll get to next). As more of the world becomes covered by cameras and more of our conversations and activities take place online, we can expect that the proportion of unstructured data will increase even further. There's a lot of undiscovered value waiting to be found, in other words.

As well as representing just a small portion of all data available, structured data is also less 'rich' than unstructured data. It offers us a more limited picture. Which is why it's often wise to use other data sources alongside structured data to enrich your insights. For example, structured data might tell you that customer satisfaction dipped in the last quarter. But it won't tell you *why*. For that, you might need to tap into some unstructured data.

On the upside, structured data is usually cheap to use, easy to store and easy to analyse with simple tools.

Unstructured and semi-structured data

Unstructured data is the term for any data that doesn't fit neatly into traditional structured formats or databases – including email conversations, website text, social media posts, video content, photos, audio recordings and so on. It's often text-heavy, but may also contain numerical data, or other types of data such as voice recordings and images. Now, thanks to AI analytics, it's becoming increasingly possible to make use of this messy, complicated data.

Semi-structured data is a cross between unstructured and structured data. This is data that may have some structure that can be used for analysis (like metadata in a photo) but lacks the strict structure found in databases or spreadsheets. For example, a tweet can be categorized by author, date, time and length, but the content itself is generally unstructured. To analyse the text in that tweet, you'd need a text analysis tool, ideally one that can carry out sentiment analytics to understand the 'mood' behind the text.

It should be clear by now that the main downside of working with unstructured data is that it's complex stuff, usually requiring specialist analytics tools. Unstructured data also tends to be much bigger than structured data, which means you need bigger and better storage, too. None of this should put you off using unstructured data. I firmly believe that it's where a lot of the undiscovered value of data lies. But it does mean you need to be very clear about what you're aiming to achieve and what data you need in order to do that.

Of course, the big advantage of unstructured and semi-structured data is that there is so much of it, and it is highly descriptive and rich in content.

Internal data

No surprises here, internal data refers to all the information your business currently has or has the potential to collect internally. It can be structured in format (like an employee database or transactional records) or it could be unstructured (like conversational data from customer service calls or feedback from employee interviews). It is your private or proprietary data that is owned by your business – and this means that only your company controls access to the data.

One downside to internal data is that you're responsible for maintaining and securing it. This costs money and, particularly in the case of personal data, there are strict data protection and privacy regulations to comply with. (Whereas, with external data, the data supplier takes on that liability for you.) Also bear in mind that internal data on its own may not provide enough information, and you may need to supplement it with external data, such as social media data. Rather like blending structured and unstructured data to get a really rich picture of what's going on, often it is necessary to combine internal data with external data to get the most useful insights.

On the upside, internal data is easy to access. You're never at the whim of a third party that can jack up prices or cut off access to the data at any time. What's more, there's real value in your internal data because it's already tailored to your business or industry. So, while you may need to look at some external data alongside your internal data to get the best results, you should never overlook it altogether.

External data

External data is the infinite array of information that exists outside of your organization. This can be publicly available (like certain government data) or privately owned by a third party (like LinkedIn), and it can also be structured or unstructured in format. Key examples of external data include social media data, Google Trends data and government census data. There are plenty of ready-made datasets available, but if you need something more bespoke you can pay a third-party provider to gather the data for you.

The obvious downside to external data is that you don't own the data and you will often have to pay for access. You'll need to weigh up the risks and the costs of accessing external data against the risks and costs of *not* having that data. Would you have to go to the trouble of creating it yourself, for example? What would happen if you didn't use that data at all? Would it stop you meeting your strategic goals?

There are some significant advantages to external data, though. The Amazons and Metas of this world are lucky enough to have huge amounts of internal data to work with. That's great for them. But many businesses can never dream of having that much data at their disposal. External data fills that gap and helps to democratize data for all types of businesses.

Exploring newer types of data

Almost everything we do these days leaves a digital footprint. And that means many new types of data are popping into existence. Let's explore some of these newer types of data and how they may prove useful to HR teams.

Just to be clear, all of these newer types of data still fit into the category of either structured, unstructured or semi-structured data, and can exist as internal or external data. I have simply grouped them together here because they represent some of the biggest leaps in data – which makes them useful considerations for any HR function.

Activity data

Activity data, which provides a record of human activities or actions (whether online or offline), can be incredibly valuable from an HR perspective. Think about all the things you do in the course of a normal day – it all generates activity data. If you wear a fitness band with a sleep tracker, like I do, even your sleep generates activity data. Then you travel to work, perhaps paying for a ticket with a bank card or touching in with a travel card. Your phone generates records of your location while you're on the move. If you make or receive a phone call on your way to work, or post a photo on Instagram, that generates data. Then you get to work and send countless emails, type hundreds or maybe thousands of words a day, and look at numerous web pages.

The sheer volume of activity data available to HR teams can be overwhelming, so it's important to always refer back to your strategic objectives and focus only on the data that helps you achieve your goals. But the real advantage of activity data is that it allows you to assess what your employees *actually* do, as opposed to what they're supposed to do, what they say they do or what you assume they do.

By tracking activity data, companies can accurately monitor individual performance, and use this information to identify top performers and those who may need help. And, of course, when you know who performs well and what characteristics top performers share, you can focus on hiring more people who match those characteristics.

One example of this comes from video game start-up Knack's collaboration with Royal Dutch Shell. Knack's video games, which were designed by a team of data scientists, psychologists and neuroscientists, aren't just about having fun – they're about measuring human potential. All sorts of factors are logged as a player participates in the games: every move they make, how they solve problems, how long they pause, and so on. This builds a thorough picture of the player's level of persistence, creativity and even intelligence, as well as their ability to prioritize tasks, and how quickly they learn from mistakes.

Royal Dutch Shell's GameChanger unit, which is charged with identifying the best business ideas from inside and outside the company, was extremely interested in the potential of these games to improve the process of identifying the best ideas. So they devised an experiment: 1,400 Shell employees who had previously proposed ideas to the GameChanger team were asked to play a couple of Knack's games. The GameChanger team then shared with Knack information on how well three-quarters of the players had fared as idea generators (whether their ideas made it all the way, for instance). Knack used this info to developed game-play profiles of the best idea generators in comparison to the weaker ones. Using information based on these top innovators' game profiles, the Knack team was then asked to guess from the remaining quarter of the players who'd had the best ideas. They did this with startling accuracy, clearly identifying those who had previously generated winning ideas based only on the way they played the games.

Based on this, Knack and Shell were able to identify the key characteristics of top idea generators, such as social intelligence and task-switching ability. This allows the GameChanger unit to devote more time to those employees whose ideas are likely to have more merit.

Conversation data

'Conversation' in this context doesn't just mean two employees having a chat around the coffee machine. It covers any conversation people may have in any format, whether it's a call with a customer, an instant message sent via phone or computer, company emails, social media posts and more. It's all conversation data.

This type of data is incredibly valuable to HR teams because it can give in-depth insights into how happy and engaged your employees really are, as well as how positive your employer brand is. Thanks to advances in analytics, conversations can now be mined for the content itself (what is said) as well as context (how it's said). This means companies can tell how happy, irritated or stressed an employee (or customer) is, or even if they're telling the truth, just by analysing the tone of their voice.

As an example, conversation data can be useful in understanding what makes an employee want to leave (or, for that matter, stay with) the company. By analysing text from open-ended questions on surveys and in exit interviews, as well as social media posts, emails and team assessments, HR teams can now accurately predict what makes an employee more likely to leave or stay with the company.

Hiring is another area that can benefit from conversation data. It's not uncommon for employers to scour social media profiles for glimpses into what potential hires are really like. This could potentially be done on a larger scale to identify the types of content and the sentiment behind things that successful employees post on social media, and use that knowledge to assess potential candidates in future.

For many companies, email is an especially rich source of conversation data, giving insights into employees' productivity, treatment of colleagues, and so on. Text analytics software is getting better and cheaper all the time, making it possible for companies to search through employees' email traffic, hunting for words, phrases or patterns of communication that are linked to certain success (or failure or attrition) metrics.

It goes without saying that there are implications to gathering and analysing conversation data. When it comes to phone calls, for instance, generally speaking, you can't record customers or employees just because you feel like it; what you're recording must be relevant to the business. You may also need to inform the parties that they are being recorded. Use of email data can also be restricted depending on where you are in the world. But we'll talk more about such pitfalls and challenges in Chapter 4.

Photo and video data

The amount of photo and video data has exploded in recent years, largely thanks to the proliferation of smartphones and the increasing use of CCTV (especially where I am in the UK). Photo and video data can be large, which can make it more expensive to store and work with. However, your company may already be collecting this data as a matter of routine (perhaps through security footage), so it may not be very difficult or expensive to find new ways to use that data more intelligently. If your company isn't collecting photo or video data already and you're interested in doing so, make sure you have a clear business case for working with this data (purely because it can be expensive).

But how could you use photo and video data? One example is using video data and video analytics to detect automatically safety violations or where employees are not wearing required personal protective equipment. Indeed, during the Covid-19 pandemic, many PPE detection tools were developed, some just using data from ordinary CCTV cameras.

Sensor data

Sensors are being built into an increasing number of products, from factory machinery to office chairs. And these sensors generate a wealth of data that can help HR departments improve their functions, including employee performance, employee safety and more.

Because sensor data tends to lack context (it's just telling you what the sensor recorded at any given time, not what might have caused that), keep in mind that it may need to be combined with another dataset to get the best results, depending on what you're trying to achieve. However, sensor data is self-generating, meaning it's very easy to capture, once the data capture tools have been put in place. Some devices, such as smart phones, contain ready-to-use sensors that can be used to the company's advantage (for example, a delivery company using their drivers' phones to track driver behaviour, for instance).

Clearly, wearable technology has a huge role to play in this type of data, and the workplace wearables market is booming. Honeywell's Connected Worker solution is just one example of this. Using a series of connected wearables sensors, the solution measures an employee's heart rate, breathing, motion and posture to assess whether they are under physical stress or in potential danger (it can detect toxic gas, for instance). This kind of technology will become more and more common in the future, especially for workers in physically demanding jobs, or those who work in dangerous or isolated locations.

Gathering the data you need

Once you know what data you need, your next step is to identify how you'll access or collect it. I'll talk more about building the right data and technology infrastructure in Chapter 14, but for now let's look at some of the general considerations around collecting data.

Sourcing data internally

A good starting point is to see whether the data you need already exists internally – or whether you have the capability to generate it yourselves, for example, by collecting data from your systems, customers or employees. As we've already seen in this chapter, you can now gather data from almost any activity undertaken by the company's employees, including test scores, interview answers, performance reviews and more.

And wherever the HR team and your company's employees are currently having conversations, there is an opportunity to collect conversation data. For example, if you operate a telephone sales department or customer service department, you can record those conversations and analyse the content and sentiment for useful insights into how staff are performing. Surveys, emails, customer feedback comments, social media platforms, and so on, all provide useful sources of conversation data.

Video and photo data can be obtained by simply starting to collect it using digital cameras. For example, retailers can use their network of CCTV cameras to analyse how the presence of staff members in certain sections of the shop floor impacts how likely a customer is to buy something. And with modern sensors being smaller and cheaper than ever (small enough to fit into an employee's badge, for instance), they can be incorporated into almost anything, from manufacturing equipment to office equipment.

Wherever possible, you want to put in place systems to collect or generate the data you need *automatically*. Whether you want to collect activity data related to employee productivity, or sensor data in a hazardous working environment, or whatever, the data collection should ideally take care of itself. The whole point of data-driven HR is to free up HR time and resource to focus on adding greater value to the company. If HR professionals are engaged in lengthy data collection exercises, this completely defeats that purpose. Of course, with any new data project, time is needed to set up, fine-tune, maintain and assess those processes, but once that is done, you should be looking to collect data with the minimum effort possible. That leaves the HR team to focus on turning that data into insights... and then acting on those insights. You'll also need to consider *when* you will collect the data. Does it need to be gathered in real-time, for example, or is it not particularly time-sensitive?

It's clear that internal data is a vital part of any data-driven HR strategy. But you may also need to combine that data with some external data to get a fuller picture that truly answers your strategic questions.

Sourcing external data

There is a wealth of external data that is already out there. Indeed, many companies exist purely to supply other companies with data. LinkedIn is perhaps one of the biggest sources of HR-related data, but there are also lots of smaller, more industry-focused data providers. So, even if you're looking for quite specialized data, there's a good chance someone out there has it.

Social media platforms are obviously key sources of useful data, and they provide a wealth of information on current, past and potential employees. You can, for example, use sentiment analysis to find out what past employees are saying about your company culture online or how happy current employees are with their working environment. Sentiment analysis can tell us a lot about users' feelings, opinions and experiences, without having to trawl through individual posts one at a time.

Other sources of HR-relevant external data may include census data, which provides a very useful source of population data, geographic data and education data. This could be useful, for example, if you were looking to set up a new office in a new location and wanted to assess the potential workforce in that area using local demographics. In addition, weather data is often used by companies to help plan staffing levels according to the number of visitors expected on a sunny weekend, for example.

When the data you want doesn't exist: The value of synthetic data in HR

One increasingly important type of data is *synthetic data*. The idea here is that, when real data isn't available – perhaps because it would be too expensive or intrusive to collect – you can create artificial data that mimics real data in every way. This can then be used to train AI algorithms and can be analysed in exactly the same way as real data can.

Synthetic data has a few advantages over real data. One is that it's comparatively cheap to 'collect'. (It isn't *collected*, of course, it's generated by algorithms, but the end result is the same.) And, somewhat counterintuitively, synthetic can sometimes represent the real world more accurately than real data, because it's not affected by biases that can influence real-world data (more on this coming up in Chapter 4).

But how is synthetic data generated? A popular technique involves generative adversarial networks that use the same algorithms as those used to create 'deepfake' images of celebrities. In the case of synthetic facial data, for example, the GAN can come up with thousands or millions of images of entirely made-up people. These images are just as useful for training facial recognition algorithms as pictures of real people, but can be generated far more quickly than real facial images can be captured, without any of the privacy or consent or bias implications.

Imagine how this approach could improve your HR datasets. If your dataset isn't very diverse, for instance, you can generate synthetic data to overcome that bias. Synthetic data can also be used to increase the sample size of HR data, leading to more accurate insights and better decision making. What's more, synthetic data is useful in HR contexts because it protects employee privacy, and allows for the testing and refinement of algorithms and models without exposing real employee data.

In other words, synthetic data enables HR professionals to work with accurate, unbiased data, leading to more equitable HR policies and practices. As such, it's well worth considering synthetic data for your use cases.

Here are just a few ways synthetic data may prove useful to HR:

- **Synthetic resumes** can be generated to test and improve resume screening algorithms. This allows you to ensure that the hiring process is free from bias while maintaining employee privacy.

- **Synthetic employee data** can be generated to test and develop HR tools such as employee performance evaluation systems, employee satisfaction surveys and employee retention models. This way, you can improve the accuracy and effectiveness of these tools without compromising employee privacy.

- **Synthetic job postings** can be created to test and improve job matching algorithms. This ensures that job openings are matched with the most qualified candidates without discriminating against any particular group of applicants.

- **Synthetic training data** can be generated to improve machine learning algorithms used in HR applications, such as chatbots, language processing and sentiment analysis. Again, this helps you develop more effective HR tools.

- **Synthetic diversity data** can be generated to test and develop diversity and inclusion policies and programmes. With such data you can analyse the effectiveness of DEI programmes without compromising employee privacy.

- **Synthetic compensation data** can be generated to test and develop pay equity models and tools. As such, you can ensure that employees are paid fairly and without any bias – again, while maintaining employee privacy.

Key takeaways

We've covered a lot of ground in this chapter, so let's recap the main points:

- There are many different types of AI-enabled analytics tools available to HR teams, including image and video analytics, text analytics, sentiment analysis and voice analytics.

- Many tools are available as off-the-shelf solutions, requiring little or no AI knowledge. The ChatGPT text generator is a great example of such a 'no-code' solution.

- Don't overlook the importance of other future technologies that are underpinned by data and AI – particularly the metaverse and blockchain. These will create many opportunities for HR to deliver a better service and employee experience.

- When it comes to data, HR teams can choose from structured data, unstructured and semi-structured data, internal data and external data. Within these categories, there are also new forms of data that can be mined for insights – specifically, activity data, conversation data, photo and video data and sensor data. It's also possible to generate synthetic data, allowing HR teams to work with unbiased, accurate data.

- Remember, no one type of data is better than another. It all comes down to knowing what it is you want to achieve and finding the data that best helps you do that. Often, the real value lies in combining different types of data and different analytics to get the richest insights.

As I've alluded to throughout this chapter, there are some significant challenges to working with data – potential bias being just one of them. In the next chapter, we delve into the challenges and pitfalls of data-driven HR.

Notes

1 J Vincent. Nvidia's AI recreates Pac-Man from scratch just by watching it being played, The Verge, 22 May 2020. www.theverge.com/2020/5/22/21266251/ nvidia-ai-gamegan-recreate-pac-man-virutal-environment (archived at https:// perma.cc/9K7J-6R2P)

2 S Alvarez. Elon Musk explains Tesla's pure vision approach to Autopilot and Full Self-Driving, Teslarati, 10 April 2021. www.teslarati.com/tesla-autopilot-fsd-camera-approach-explained-elon-musk (archived at https://perma.cc/ NH5X-HAVE)

3 D Peck. They're watching you at work, The Atlantic, December 2013. www. theatlantic.com/magazine/archive/2013/12/theyre-watching-you-at-work/ 354681 (archived at https://perma.cc/KVT4-3PUX)

4 F Hersey. South Korea's digital identity blockchain prepares to add new credentials, go international, Biometric Update, 27 December 2022. www. biometricupdate.com/202212/south-koreas-digital-identity-blockchain-prepares-to-add-new-credentials-go-international (archived at https://perma.cc/93DZ-2CPS)

Challenges and 04
pitfalls of AI and
data-driven HR

Data and AI can bring great rewards. But they also bring challenges, particularly when it comes to the use of highly valuable personal data. Which is why every organization needs to practise good governance when it comes to data and AI.

Practising good governance means being aware of the legal requirements concerning every aspect of your data- and AI-related activities, and ensuring that you're operating in an open, ethical, and transparent manner. It also extends to having policies in place to determine exactly who has access to data, and who is responsible for maintaining the quality and accuracy of that data.

Assuming your organization has a data and AI governance policy already in place (and it really should), you need to ensure your HR activities operate within the scope of that policy. But you may also need to put in place policies that are specific to your HR remit. This may include defining exactly who owns the various people-related data within the organization and who is accountable for various aspects of the data (such as updating data and making sure data is accurate). It's also a good idea to appoint a data and AI champion from within your team to coordinate with others in the company on issues of governance, quality and privacy.

In this chapter, we'll explore this notion of data and AI governance, including the pitfalls and challenges you may encounter along the way.

Understanding the value of data

Good data governance is about treating data as a valuable business asset that must be protected. The HR function in particular deals with data that is very sensitive and extremely valuable. Why? Because it is *personal data*.

Personal data is any information that's related to an identifiable person. If we think about the average HR team, some of the data routinely collected on employees (and potential employees) includes:

- Personal information, like name, contact details, date of birth, gender, nationality and social security number.
- Financial information, including bank account details, tax information and other financial records.
- Employment history, such as previous employers, job titles, employment dates and reasons for leaving.
- Health information, which may include disability status, medical records and workers' compensation claims.
- Criminal records, including arrest records, convictions and other criminal history information.
- Compensation and benefits data, such as salaries, bonuses and healthcare costs.
- Education and qualifications, like degrees, certifications, institutions attended and dates of completion.
- Job application data, for instance, resumes, cover letters, references and interview notes.
- Recruitment and selection data, including assessment scores, background checks and hiring decisions.
- And performance metrics, such as sales numbers, customer satisfaction scores and productivity rates.

Clearly this is all extremely sensitive data, and as such, it carries a heavy governance burden. Depending on where you are in the world, there are likely to be strict regulations that govern the use of personal data (more on this coming up), obviously with a key emphasis on protecting that data, but also gaining consent to use the data.

You will need to ensure that everyone who comes into contact with your people-related data is aware of the value of this data, and the associated governance issues. They must be aware of the privacy and permissions issues surrounding that data. And they must be aware of the rules and procedures for how that data can be used. Basically, if your people do not give data the respect it deserves – if they don't treat data as a precious business asset – it can very quickly become a liability.

With that liability in mind, let's dwell on the biggest risks that may apply to your people-related data.

The biggest data-related challenges

Please do keep in mind that these are all huge topics in their own right – and regulations and the threat landscape are constantly changing. Specialist legal and technical advice is therefore recommended.

Legal and regulatory compliance

HR departments must comply with various data protection laws, such as the General Data Protection Regulation (GDPR) in Europe, the Health Insurance Portablility and Accountability Act (HIPPA) in the US, and the California Consumer Privacy Act (CCPA). Failure to protect employee data can result in penalties, fines and legal action – not to mention the reputational risk that comes with a data breach.

Data privacy laws vary greatly around the world. The EU arguably has some of the most stringent rules, and in the US it can vary from state to state. It's therefore vital that any HR team gathering sensitive personal data makes sure they're operating within the laws of their country.

In Europe, the GDPR is designed to enhance data protection and the right to privacy for EU citizens, giving them greater control over their personal data and how it is used. It is also implemented into law in the UK.

The GDPR states that companies can only use personal data for the *express purpose* for which it was given. And that includes the personal data of employees. Consent is therefore a critical pillar of GDPR. Employees must explicitly *opt in* to allow a company to use their personal data, and they must be made fully aware of how that data will be used. This can be clarified through a simple data privacy statement distributed to employees. Crucially, you can then only use the data for the purpose for which it was handed over.

The GDPR also sets out strict mandates around reporting the theft or loss of personal data. So, in the event of any breach that affects employee data, you will need to inform the supervising authority (in the UK that's the Information Commissioner's Office) within a maximum of 72 hours. You'll also have to inform those individuals whose data is affected.

You may also be affected by rules that govern the transfer of data from one country to another. Say, if you're a European company but you have a US office, or your data analytics provider is based in the US, you'll be affected by GDPR data transfer rules.

In the US, regulation around the use of personal data may be a little less stringent, but there are still many things that can trip a company up. As Felix

Wu, Professor of Law at the Benjamin N Cardozo School of Law, once told me, 'Unlike Europe, the US does not have comprehensive privacy regulation, but this may actually make things more difficult for companies, which must comply with a patchwork of varying state and federal laws.' California, for instance, has the CCPA, which is similar to GDPR. Various (but not all) states have similar laws, drawing upon parts of GDPR or even the CCPA. But the specifics vary across state lines, making it difficult for organizations that operate nationally. That said, the US does have nationwide data privacy and data protection laws for certain industries. A good example is HIPPA, which governs how personal health information can be used. Basically, wherever you are in the world, specialist legal advice is a must.

Even working within these regulations, employers can still gather (with consent) huge amounts of useful data. In the relatively strict European Union, for instance, employers can monitor staff emails, other electronic messages and the websites visited during work hours, providing they have good reason for doing so and have consent. This doesn't give you carte blanche to read all employee communications just because you feel like it, but it is allowed when you have legitimate reason for monitoring employees' communications on company resources (again, with consent and after informing employees of how you intend to use that data). Telephone calls may also be monitored for business purposes (with consent, of course).

What this means for HR teams is that any monitoring of employee communications must be clearly explained in a privacy policy, employee handbook or contract and you should get employee consent for that monitoring. You need to make it very clear what data you're gathering in terms of emails, instant messages, website usage, etc. and *why* you're doing that. If there isn't a clear business reason for gathering the data – for example, to improve performance – you shouldn't be doing it.

I would also steer well clear of messages that are obviously of a very personal nature and are not related to the business. Essentially, you should seek to strike a balance between the privacy of your employees and the needs of the business, and be transparent about what you're doing at all times. Which brings me to…

Ethical issues and the need for transparency

As well as sitting on the right side of the law, you also need to ensure that your data usage sits within the ethical boundaries set by the company. Say your organization espouses a culture of openness and honesty, you can't then have your data-driven HR activities fly in the face of that culture. Clumsily implemented or poorly communicated data projects can do a lot of damage when it comes to employee trust and morale. So it's important not to gloss over this aspect of data-driven HR.

On the whole, though, we're all getting a lot more used to the wealth of data being collected and generated about us. When we sign up for a free email service, we acknowledge the email provider's right to read those emails. When we use an app, we agree to the provider's right to use our location data, among other things. We're all getting used to our everyday activities being tracked.

This doesn't mean generating or gathering people-related data can be a free-for-all. As I've emphasized, you must have a clear business case for collecting data on your employees and this must be properly communicated. Transparency is one of the key pieces of advice I give to every company I work with. Another is emphasizing the *benefits* of data. You ideally want to achieve widespread buy-in for the use of data, from the top-level executives to front-line employees. And it's easy for people to get on board with data when they understand how it will benefit the company and them as employees. Just as hundreds of millions of people are seemingly happy for Google to scan their emails in return for a free email service, your employees are more likely to be happy with you using their data if they understand that information will be used to improve their working environment, for instance.

In other words, transparency is vital, but so is *adding value* for employees. People are far happier for their data to be used when they feel they're getting something valuable in return, whether it's better working conditions, more effective management, a safer environment, or whatever.

The key to success in data-driven HR is therefore to be open about how you want to use the data you collect, to operate ethically and offer genuine value to your employees in return. When you provide value and can demonstrate a clear business case, most people will be happy, especially if the data is anonymized (more on this coming up).

So far we've talked about the ethical and legal risks around data. But there are also some major technology risks around data.

The devastating impact of data breaches

The downside of generating more and more data is that it introduces new vulnerabilities to the organization, by creating more data that someone could potentially steal. These days, it seems like barely a week goes by without reports of yet another large-scale loss or theft of personal data. Data breaches can lead to huge losses for businesses, in terms of legal costs and financial compensation, as well as the damage done to the company's reputation.

And if you think that no one would be interested in stealing your employee-related data (as opposed to, say, customer credit card details), think again. As we've already seen in this chapter, the wealth of people-related data available to the average HR team contains personally identifiable information that's valuable to criminals. Names, addresses, social security numbers, banking details… if this data got into the wrong hands, it could clearly lead to identity theft, causing significant harm to affected employees. It could also seriously tarnish your employer brand.

Another threat to be aware of is ransomware attacks – where a virus infects the system and makes valuable data unusable unless a ransom is paid. Phishing attacks are often the way in to the company system. And now, with powerful AIs like ChatGPT (see Chapter 3), the danger is attackers can create authentic-sounding, highly personalized phishing messages very easily.

There is also a rising threat from the Internet of Things, and its ever-expanding network of connected devices. The theory is simple – the more devices that are connected to the internet means more possible attack vectors for intruders who want data. The how and the why is a bit more complicated – what benefit would an attacker gain from taking control of a sensor on a factory machine, for instance? Well, aside from causing mischief (which is certainly the main motive for a good deal of hacking activity) the likelihood is that they want to use it to take advantage of network vulnerabilities which would allow them to get at the real jackpot – other devices on the network such as PCs or phones which are far more likely to hold sensitive and valuable information. Any HR team using IoT-related devices to gather data needs to take their security very seriously, and apply the same level of security (passwords, regular system updates, etc.) as you would for any other device.

Defending your data

When you're dealing with personal data, you're responsible for its protection. You're responsible for preventing data loss and breaches.

You can't properly protect data if you aren't entirely sure what data you have. Therefore, an important first step is being aware of exactly what people-related data you have, including where that data resides, exactly what data is involved (critically, does it include personally identifiable information?), who that data is divulged to, how that data is processed or analysed and how it's then used within the organization. Don't forget to consider any data that may be used or processed by third parties (a payroll company, for instance) or anything that's stored with off-site data providers or in the cloud.

Another important step is to follow a strategy of *data minimization*. In other words, don't collect every scrap of data that you possibly can 'just in case'. Rather, you should seek to gather only the very essential data, i.e. data that can help meaningfully improve the company and add value. Indeed, these days, data privacy regulations often restrict data collection to a minimum. The GDPR, for instance, insists that any personal data collected must be 'adequate, relevant and limited to the minimum necessary for the purposes for which the data are processed'.

Wherever you are in the world, restricting the amount of data you collect to the minimum necessary is a wise approach, but you can also take steps to *anonymize* personal data by removing any personally identifiably markers. This way, it can be used for analytic purposes without being linked to an identifiable person.

Say, for example, you're analysing the performance of sales colleagues to identify the key traits of successful salespeople in order to inform future recruitment decisions. In this case, what you're really aiming to do is hire the best talent for your sales team and remove some of the guesswork from the recruitment process. And if that's the goal, do you really need the data you gather to identify individual sales colleagues?

You must also take measures to ensure the data is secured, especially when it isn't anonymized. There are certain safeguards any business can put in place to secure data and prevent data breaches. Such measures can include:

1 Encrypting your data, thereby rendering it far less useful to anyone who might want to steal it. Homomorphic encryption is an excellent option. Here, data is encrypted in such a way that it can be analysed while remaining in its encrypted form – even the analytical algorithms don't 'see' the unencrypted data.

2 Restricting access to personal data to only those who need access.

3 Having systems in place to detect and stop breaches while they are happening.

4 Training your staff so they never give away secure information and are aware of threats such as phishing emails.

Do keep in mind that data security is a specialist field and it's always a good idea to consult with a data security expert, either inside or outside your organization.

AI pitfalls

So far, we've focused on issues surrounding data. But the use of AI also creates unique challenges – some related to the data itself, and others related more to ethical questions around AI. Let's explore these AI-related pitfalls in more detail.

The thorny issue of AI ethics

AI truly has the potential to change business and wider society in ways that we can't yet imagine. The fundamental change that we're seeing right now is that, instead of only carrying out repetitive tasks – such as applying formulas to figures in a spreadsheet (which computers already do exceptionally well) – intelligent machines are increasingly being used to make decisions.

Inevitably, this will include decisions that affect the people who work for your organization. Amazon, for instance, has used AI algorithms to automatically track and fire hundreds of fulfilment centre employees.[1] This is the tip of the iceberg as we grapple with huge ethical questions around decision making in machines. One commonly used example in AI ethics is how should a self-driving car act when it has to decide whether it should crash into a pedestrian or a brick wall (potentially injuring its own driver)?

The truth is, AI can be used for enormous good, but it can also be used for nefarious purposes. Machine vision can detect cancerous growth in medical scan images but it can also be used by totalitarian regimes to carry out surveillance on their citizens. Natural language processing like ChatGPT makes it easier than ever for humans to interact with machines, but it can also be used to orchestrate scams and phishing attacks by impersonating people.

Yes, these are extreme examples, but if you're deploying AI systems within your organization you'll likely have to make some ethical choices. It's therefore important to think about how your use of AI fits with the company's overall culture and ethics. What's more, because AI systems rely on data, you have to contend with the same issues around consent and privacy. You have to gain consent for any work you do with personal data and ensure your AI use stays on the right side of the law.

But there's often a difference between what's legal and what's ethical. Amazon's highly automated firing of employees is not likely to be illegal. But ethical? You can make a strong argument that giving machines the power to make decisions that massively impact employees' lives is ethically iffy at best. And it's far from clear that the employees involved ever gave consent for AI to have this much power over their lives.

Even if you aren't giving intelligent machines the power to make such life-impacting decisions, but merely to run processes more efficiently, care must be taken. In 2018, IT contractor Ibrahim Diallo arrived at his Los Angeles office to find he couldn't get in because his security pass had been revoked. When he managed to gain access, he couldn't log into his computer or any of the systems he needed to do his job, and shortly afterwards security guards arrived to escort him from the building. His pay was also stopped. Neither his manager or any other senior member of staff knew what had happened, but after being forced to work from home for three weeks they eventually found that an HR error had mistakenly flagged him up as having been dismissed. At that point automated systems kicked into action, which had no way of being manually overridden! The stress he experienced, and his leaders' inability to do anything about it, caused him to leave the company and find work elsewhere.[2]

And what about when employees aren't fired by AI, but *because* of AI? As more responsibilities are given over to machines, this changes the work that humans do, and renders some jobs obsolete. The World Economic Forum predicts that 85 million human roles will have been automated into redundancy by 2025. However, over the same period, the boom in AI and other advanced, automated technology will lead to the creation of 97 million new roles.[3] So AI and automation will create more jobs than are displaced.

But that doesn't mean automation isn't an ethical concern, as far as replacing human jobs is concerned. You must still consider the impact of AI, automation and data initiatives on your human workforce. Is there a risk that anyone will become redundant? If so, can they be reskilled and redeployed elsewhere in the organization? (Read more about reskilling and preparing the organization for changing skill needs in Chapter 6.)

Crucially, is there a danger that people would become redundant anyway, regardless of whether you use AI? For example, would failing to deploy AI create a situation in which your company is no longer competitive or viable? There are many situations where *not* using AI is an unsound strategy. If problems exist in your company that could be tackled with AI, do you have an ethical obligation to use it?

I can't answer that question for you. But I do recommend that every organization looking to roll out AI should set up some kind of 'ethics council'. The size and scale of your council and the amount of resources dedicated to it will depend on the size of the organization. But the important thing is to have someone who has the responsibility of considering all the issues raised here and how they impact your initiatives.

If you want to understand more about AI ethics, I highly recommend reading the Organization for Economic Co-operation and Development (OECD) AI Principles, which are designed to promote the ethical use of AI.[4]

Transparency around AI

Just as with data, transparency is vital when you're working with AI. It's really important to explain how and why AI is being used. After all, if intelligent machines are going to be making decisions that potentially impact the people in your organization, then you should at least be able to explain the decision-making processes used by the machines.

In AI circles, this is known as the 'black box' problem, whereby algorithms can be so complex that it's very difficult for humans to precisely understand how they do what they do. In other words, 'We know it works, but we don't understand *how* it works!' This is compounded by the fact that some AI is deliberately made opaque by those who sell it, in order to prevent it being easily copied.

You want to strive for 'AI explainability', so people at every level of the organization can understand how AI is used and how it might impact them. If you're using off-the-shelf software, for example, choose a provider that explains how their AI works. It's also a good idea to have a grievance process in place, whereby employees can raise concerns if they feel they've been treated unfairly because of AI-related decisions.

Remember when we talked about getting buy-in for collecting data, so that employees understand how the use of data benefits them, their job, and the organization as a whole? The exact same thing goes for AI. So, as well as being transparent about how and why you're using AI, do be sure to sell the benefits as well.

The environmental cost

I can't talk about AI and data concerns without mentioning the environmental impact. All that computing power needed to train and run AI systems burns up a lot of electricity. As an example, according to estimates, training OpenAI's GPT-3 language model took about as much electricity as 120 US homes would consume in a year.[5]

Of course, AI creates the potential to drive efficiencies that can lead to reductions in environmental impact – think of smart home thermostats, for example, which help homeowners use energy more efficiently and in turn cut emissions. It's not as clear-cut as saying 'AI is terrible for the environment', but the environmental impact certainly warrants consideration.

A quick word on AI and ownership

IP rights and ownership is another issue that requires consideration. This is simple enough – you just need to be sure you have the rights to use any algorithms you're employing, either under licence from your AI provider, or because you've developed and own them outright yourselves.

Bias and the importance of 'clean' data

Now we bring it full circle back to data. Because AI algorithms are only as good as the data they are trained on. A key part of governance is therefore making sure that the data you are using is as clean as possible. What do I mean by 'clean'? I mean two things: data that is of high quality, and data that's free from bias. Let's look at both issues.

Working with high-quality data

In essence, data quality refers to a standard of measures that can be used to assess whether the data is fit for purpose. These measures are all equally important for data quality:

Measurements for data quality

- *Consistency:* This first measure means that the data in a dataset is all recorded and collated in the same way. For example, if you have multiple fields in a record, then every record should have all of the fields complete. Fields should be used the same way across every record, and if we 'know' something about one piece of information in the dataset, we should know it about every piece of information, so we are always able to use the data together.

- *Accuracy:* This means that the data is error-free. In the case of automatically collected data, the tools or sensors that have been used to collect the data must be audited so that you know they're working properly. Of course, errors can occur with human-inputted data too, so we have to ensure that those with data-entry responsibilities are trained and aware of the need for accuracy.

- *Uniqueness:* This means that there are no duplicate entries. If the same piece of data is recorded more than once, it's very likely that your database will start to become inaccurate.

- *Validity:* Validity is a way of measuring whether every record or piece of data in a database is fit for the purpose it's intended for. For example, are dates all stored in the correct format, and are all of the figures stored in the same way?

- *Timeliness:* Timeliness measures whether your data is likely to be relevant, with regard to the time at which it was collected. Some processes need only be measured very occasionally in order to monitor and understand them. Others need to be measured much more frequently. And for those operations that require real-time datasets, measurements must be taken and recorded with a delay that is as close to zero as possible.

- *Completeness:* Finally, completeness is a measurement of how much of the total availability of data on a subject is captured in your dataset. The greater the completeness of your dataset, the more grounded in reality your insights will be.

If you want to ensure you're working with high-quality data, it's really important you audit your data using these metrics.

The problem of data bias

The second element of 'clean data' is bias, by which we mean data that is not truly representative of the data subject. Usually this relates to the way in which the data was collected. For example, if you are trying to measure customer satisfaction using feedback forms, and you only send the forms to customers who have left positive reviews, your data is going to be inherently biased.

With the huge and complex datasets used in AI initiatives, the potential for bias to creep in is ever-present. This is a big challenge for many data initiatives, because biased data means your insights will not be informed by objective reality. In fact, preventing bias (or at least reducing the damage it can cause) is seen by AI thought leaders as one of the biggest challenges our society will have to overcome, if the potential of AI is to be realized.

Biased data can be the result of poor data quality, as outlined above, but sometimes, even if your data measures up well against all of the quality metrics, bias can still creep in. This is because bias isn't necessarily 'wrong', in terms of whether the data is accurate, unique, valid or timely. It might just mean you aren't casting your net widely enough in order to get diverse measurements, viewpoints or opinions. As a result, the models and simulations you build won't represent the real world.

There are very serious implications to data bias. In the US, when facial recognition systems used by police forces to identify suspects in crowds were audited, it was found that young, female, black citizens were far more likely than any other age group to be misidentified.[6] When applied to people in this demographic, the accuracy rate of the algorithm was found to be 34 per cent lower than with other groups. If left unchecked, this could clearly lead to higher rates of wrongful stops, arrests or searches of young black women.

Recruitment is one area where data bias can cause real problems for HR teams. Noel Sharkey, a Professor of AI and Robotics at the University of Sheffield, has said that datasets used by recruitment algorithms that he has studied are so riddled with bias that they simply shouldn't be used until they can be regulated and audited with the same degree of thoroughness as is used for data in pharmaceutical trials.[7] In 2018, Amazon stopped using a machine learning algorithm that was designed to assess job applicants, after discovering that it was 'sexist'. Because far fewer women than men had applied to work for the company over the previous 10 years, the dataset that the algorithm used was found to discriminate against women, passing them over for opportunities for no reason other than the fact it did not have enough data on female applicants for these roles.[8]

Clearly, you will need to take a careful look at the data and AI algorithms you use to check for possible bias. Ask yourself questions like, 'Does this data exclude certain groups or skew in favour of certain groups?' and 'How does this algorithm make decisions?' (There's that explainability issue again.) And remember, as we saw in Chapter 3, synthetic data can help to overcome inherent bias in data by creating new data that's more representative than your existing data.

To make things even more complicated, sometimes it might be appropriate to introduce bias into a system deliberately, in order to compensate for social factors that lean towards unfairness or intolerance. In recent years, Microsoft and IBM have both released AI-powered chatbots that later had to be adapted (deactivated, in Microsoft's case) to stop them acting in a racist and abusive manner. This was because they were learning how to converse based on social media interactions which, of course, can often be racist or abusive themselves. So they had no choice but to introduce an element of deliberate bias into the system – in this case, telling the bot that it shouldn't be learning from racist or abusive data. Of course, this inevitably means that the data the bots learn from is less representative of real life. However, as it's clearly unacceptable for a bot representing a company like IBM to be using racist language and quoting Hitler, there wasn't a lot of choice! Balancing up the harm that can be done by introducing biased data against the harm done by excluding it is an essential part of the process of governance, too.

We must also remember that AI, particularly when it comes to something like recruitment, can help to *overcome* human biases. A well-trained algorithm working with unbiased data will be less prone to prejudice and bias than many human decision makers. So despite the risk of bias, AI has much to offer when it comes to making better, fairer decisions.

Key takeaways

Let's briefly recap some of the main lessons from this chapter:

- HR teams deal with highly personal, sensitive data – data that is valuable to the organization, but also attractive to hackers. Good data governance is essential.

- Data governance involves working in line with data protection regulations, having clear data policies in place that govern the use of data, and being open and transparent with employees about what data is collected (with consent) and how it is being used. Data regulations vary around the world (and from state to state in the US) so do seek specialist advice for your jurisdiction.

- It's vital you protect data from threats such as ransomware attacks. To protect your data, you first need to be crystal clear about what data you have, and who has access to it (including third parties). You should also encrypt data, restrict access to only those who need it, have systems in place to detect and stop breaches and train staff to be alert to threats. You should also follow good practices around data minimization and anonymization wherever possible.

- AI has its own ethical and technical challenges. For one thing, you should be able to explain to employees *how* AI systems make decisions (thereby avoiding the 'black box' problem). You must also be aware of the potential for bias to creep in, and take steps to counter bias in your data and AI systems (for example, using synthetic data). Plus, your data needs to be 'clean' (accurate, complete, etc.).

Another challenge with data and AI is working out how best to use it in your organization! With so many potential uses, prioritizing your use cases is no easy feat. In the next chapter, we'll explore how to find the most strategic uses for data and AI in your HR function.

Notes

1 V Tangermann. Amazon used an AI to automatically fire low-productivity workers, Futurism, 26 April 2019. futurism.com/amazon-ai-fire-workers (archived at https://perma.cc/N8SK-TZNT)

2 J Wakefield. The man who was fired by a machine, BBC News, 21 June 2018. www.bbc.co.uk/news/technology-44561838 (archived at https://perma.cc/R4FU-J6E4)

3 M Kande and M Sonmez. Don't fear AI. It will lead to long-term job growth, World Economic Forum, 26 October 2020. www.weforum.org/agenda/2020/10/dont-fear-ai-it-will-lead-to-long-term-job-growth (archived at https://perma.cc/LQ4P-CNMH)

4 OECD. OECD AI principles overview, OECD, May 2019. oecd.ai/en/ai-principles (archived at https://perma.cc/97VP-NQH2)

5 J Saul and D Bass. Artificial intelligence is booming – so is its carbon footprint, Bloomberg, 9 March 2023. www.bloomberg.com/news/articles/2023-03-09/how-much-energy-do-ai-and-chatgpt-use-no-one-knows-for-sure (archived at https://perma.cc/EC33-4UBB)

6 A Najibi. Racial discrimination in face recognition technology, Harvard University, 24 October 2020. sitn.hms.harvard.edu/flash/2020/racial-discrimination-in-face-recognition-technology (archived at https://perma.cc/5EAQ-5PV2)

7 N Sharkey. AI expert calls for end to UK use of 'racially biased' algorithms, *The Guardian*, 12 December 2019. www.theguardian.com/technology/2019/dec/12/ai-end-uk-use-racially-biased-algorithms-noel-sharkey (archived at https://perma.cc/4WYH-TZ62)

8 J Dastin. Amazon scraps secret AI recruiting tool that showed bias against women, Reuters, 11 October 2018. www.reuters.com/article/us-amazon-com-jobs-automation-insight-idUSKCN1MK08G (archived at https://perma.cc/MRZ6-PPPQ)

Finding the right ways to use data and AI in HR 05

In order to get the most out of data and AI, it's vital you act strategically. You need a strategy that maps out how HR can best use data and AI to help drive the business forward. In practice, this means looking at the work that HR functions do, and how data and AI can improve those processes. With this in mind, you can identify your priority objectives (within the context of the organization's wider goals, of course), pinpoint the data you need, and so on.

This chapter sets out the process of creating a strategy for intelligent HR. But why is strategy so important when it comes to data and AI?

Why it all starts with strategy

As we saw in Chapter 2, the explosion in data is affecting almost every area of our lives, including work. We now live in a world in which the amount of data being generated every day – even every second – is, frankly, astonishing. And when it comes to what we should do with all this data, I've found that many companies, or functions within organizations, fall into one of two camps: some are so eager to ride the data train, they dive in and start collecting all kinds of data simply *because they can*, with no thought as to how that data benefits the business; others prefer to bury their heads in the sand, often because they're so overwhelmed they don't know where to start.

The same can be said of AI. So far in this book, we've seen just a taste of the cool things that organizations can do with AI (there are plenty more examples coming up in Part Two), but it should be clear already that the possibilities are evolving fast. And with AI-driven advancements like blockchain and the metaverse coming into focus, things are only going to accelerate.

I don't say that to put you off or intimidate you. Only to emphasize that, with the technology landscape changing so rapidly, it's easy to get lost in the weeds. Which is why it's so important to stay focused on your most pressing goals – and how you can best use data and AI to achieve those goals. This is where strategy comes in.

Having a clear strategy will also help you avoid overdosing on data. Given the risks and pitfalls around data – especially personal data – it's never a good idea to start collecting huge amounts of people-related data that you don't really need. I always say that the power of data isn't in the impressive amount of data you can collect or the super-cool AI analytics that are available. The power of data lies in *how you use it*. It's about how you use the insights that you glean from the data to improve decisions, better understand your employees, optimize operations and add value to the company. Therefore, you need to be very clear about what it is you want to achieve, and what kind of data and AI analytics will help you achieve that. Creating a robust data strategy will help you develop and maintain a laser-like focus on your goals and map out your next steps.

But where do you start?

Begin with your objectives

Finding the best uses for data and AI means identifying the areas where data and analytics can provide the most value for the organization.

Understanding potential uses of data and AI in HR

Within the context of HR's role in the organization, there are three main ways in which data and AI can add value to the business. They are:

- generating better HR insights to aid decision making across the organization
- delivering a better service for employees (and candidates)
- driving efficiencies in HR services

Let's briefly explore each one.

Generating better HR insights to aid decision making across the organization

Here, we're talking about getting information to the people within the organization who need it most, providing people-related reporting, helping the business understand what's going on now, informing decision makers about people-related challenges that may be on the horizon (using AI's predictive capabilities to create early warning systems), and helping the business plan for the future (addressing skills gaps, for example).

As an example, networking hardware company Juniper Networks uses LinkedIn data and analytics to analyse where top-performing employees come from – but also where they go when they leave the company. This helps the company better understand career paths and, in turn, make better decisions on how to attract and retain talent.[1]

We'll delve more into the topic of generating insights in Chapter 6, but suffice to say that data and AI are absolutely fundamental to this process of generating better, more forward-thinking insights.

Delivering a better service for employees (and candidates)

The HR function is all about serving the people who work in the organization – providing a great recruitment service, awesome training and development opportunities, a thoughtful wellbeing offering, a safe working environment and all those other ways in which HR serves workers. HR teams can use data and AI to make these services better, create a richer employee experience and add more value for employees at all stages of the employee lifecycle. Walmart, for example, uses AI to help employees find the right medical provider for their needs.[2] We'll explore plenty more examples from various HR services in Part Two.

Driving efficiencies in HR services

AI in particular has much to offer HR teams who want to improve the efficiency of their services. So we're talking about things like automating certain HR processes (using chatbots, for example), using AI in onboarding, using metaverse environments to make training more immersive, and so on. Again, we'll explore these various HR services in Part Two. But as a quick example, Johnson & Johnson has used an AI automated writing tool called Textio to scan for unconscious bias in its job postings. Using this tool, Johnson & Johnson recruiters uncovered that the language in many of their job postings skewed masculine – but thanks to some simple AI-powered edits, the company saw a 9 per cent increase in female applicants.[3]

When thinking about how best to use data and AI, I suggest you keep these three branches of HR activity firmly in mind. They should serve as a useful starting point when defining your strategic objectives.

Now it's time to define your strategic HR objectives

How can you best use data and AI in your organization? Well, it depends on your specific HR challenges and objectives.

What is it you most want to achieve as an HR function? Maybe you want to improve recruitment and selection, reduce turnover, boost employee performance, enhance your training and development offering... Every organization is different. Some HR teams may, for example, face greater operational challenges, while other companies are suffering significant morale problems and need to develop a better understanding of their people. You can't begin to look at data and AI options until you've identified your most pressing goals and challenges.

Of course, the best kind of HR data strategy is directly linked to the organization's wider objectives and, in effect, should cascade down from those corporate objectives. To put it another way, you're not just looking at HR-specific goals and challenges, but also how you can add value to the organization and help deliver the company's vision.

Therefore, your organization's overarching strategic plan should inform your thinking at this stage. In an ideal world, your organization's strategic plan would be a concise, simple document that anyone in the organization can read and understand – something like a 'plan on a page' that clearly sets out where the organization needs to go. However, this isn't always the case and I recognize that some organizational strategic plans are overly long and complex, making it difficult to determine what actions need to be taken. Whatever your company's strategy looks like, it should set out intended outcomes for the company, including financial and non-financial objectives, and (hopefully) the core activities and enablers that will lead to those outcomes being achieved. If you struggle to understand this from the company's strategic plan, have a discussion with your leadership team before going any further. It's vital you understand where the business as a whole wants to go.

Say, for example, your company has a corporate objective to become a top-three provider of specific consultancy services within the next three years. That will translate into various HR-related actions such as assessing and optimizing your employer brand in order to attract the best talent. In this case, the biggest opportunities for data-driven HR are likely to lie in generating better insights and delivering an awesome recruitment and on-boarding service.

Basically, this stage is all about identifying where the biggest data- and AI-related opportunities lie for your HR function, based on your HR objectives and wider corporate objectives.

How many objectives is too many?

I cannot recommend strongly enough that you keep this objectives phase simple. Don't be tempted to create a list of 100 HR objectives that cover everything you could possibly want to achieve. Instead, focus only on core objectives. After all, you can't create a robust data strategy if you aren't crystal clear on what exactly you need to achieve and, in turn, what areas or activities you need to focus on to achieve those aims. A list of 100 nice-to-have objectives will lead to a very muddled (and probably very expensive) strategy that delivers little real value.

I recommend identifying around three top priority objectives as a starting point. These should represent your most pressing HR challenges, or goals that will add the most value to the organization, based on its overarching strategic objectives.

Some companies and functions like to map out their objectives as a simple 'plan on a page' – a one-pager that visualizes where the organization (or function within the organization) is heading. This certainly isn't essential, but it does make it easier to communicate your goals, and serves as a useful document to refer back to in future. But a simple list of objectives will do.

With your objectives firmly in mind, you're ready to create your HR data and AI strategy. Which brings us to…

Creating your strategy

To be clear, you're not looking to create a lengthy strategy document that no one ever reads because it's so complex. A good HR data strategy can be easily broken down into a few simple sections that determine what it is you want to do with data and AI. The following six questions will help you understand and really clarify what you want to do, and, as such, they form the basis of any good data strategy.

But before we get into the questions themselves, keep in mind that you may need some expert help to pull your strategy together and put it into practice – particularly from your in-house IT professionals and data scientists, who will advise you on which data and AI solutions are technically feasible. If your organization is small and doesn't have the data knowledge and IT expertise in-house, there are many data consultants who will help you determine the best course of action for your needs.

As well as the IT team, it's also important to involve other stakeholders from across the organization, particularly business leaders, to ensure that your intended uses are aligned with the organization's objectives. Remember, the right use cases for data and AI in HR will depend on the organization's needs, so you want to take a collaborative approach to creating your data strategy. Plus, if your company has an ethics council (see Chapter 4), you'll want to work with them to ensure your chosen uses are ethical.

Now let's get into the six questions or steps that you can use as the foundation of your data and AI strategy…

1. What questions do we need to answer to achieve our goals?

Surprisingly, a good data strategy doesn't start with data. It starts with your unanswered business questions. Many of the organizations and functions I work with tend to ask for as much data as possible – not because they plan to do very clever analytics, but because they don't know what data they really need. By pinpointing your unanswered questions, you can hone in on the data you need most.

So, having set out what it is you want to achieve (your objectives, from earlier in the chapter), you now need to pin down the big questions you must answer if you're going to deliver those goals. Some of the questions might have been identified already as you worked out your objectives, while others will need careful thought at this stage.

Defining these questions helps you identify exactly what you need to know. And by making sure your questions are linked to your company's priorities, you can ensure they're the most strategically important questions, rather than asking every little 'nice to know but not essential' question.

2. What data do I need to answer those questions or solve those problems?

Look at each question you identified in step 1 and then think about the data you need in order to answer those questions. Much of that data may come from within the company itself, but you may also need to make use of external data providers.

Establish what data you already have access to (from HR systems, employee surveys, performance metrics, etc.) and what you don't yet have access to. For the data you don't have access to, do you need to partner with an external provider or can you set up new data collection methods to gather the data internally? Circle back to Chapter 3 for more on the data itself.

3. How will we analyse that data?

Having pinned down your information needs and the data you require, next you need to look at your analytics requirements, i.e. how you will analyse that data and turn it into valuable insights that help you answer your questions and achieve your goals.

As we saw in Chapter 3, much of the promise of data lies in using machine learning to analyse unstructured data, like email conversations, social media posts, video content, voice recordings, and so on. Combining this messy and complex data with other more traditional data, like KPIs or sales data, is where a lot of the value lies. And remember, these days there are many off-the-shelf AI analytics solutions that will help you extract value from data. Again, you can circle back to Chapter 3 for a refresher on the different types of analytics, but we'll also explore analytics more in Chapter 6.

4. How will we report and present insights from the data?

Data is only really valuable if you can turn it into insights and actionable knowledge. To put it another way, data is absolutely useless if it isn't presented to the *right people* in the *right way* at the *right time*, so that the *right actions* can be taken. This is how businesses gain competitive advantage.

Perhaps the most important thing to remember at this stage is to keep your target audience in mind. Therefore, you need to define the audience for your data (i.e. who requires insights from the data?) and work out how best to get that information to them. The HR team itself may be the largest audience, but no doubt you will also need to present insights to others elsewhere in the organization, including the leadership team and managers across the business. Indeed, as we saw earlier in the chapter, communicating insights from data and aiding decision making across the business is one of the critical ways for HR teams to add value through data and AI. We'll delve into this in more detail in Chapter 6.

What's the best way to disseminate insights to the people that need them? Options for reporting and presenting insights vary from fancy dashboards with real-time data through to simple reports with key insights presented as visuals. The right option for you depends on what you're measuring, who needs to know about it, and how you usually communicate across the company.

However you decide to disseminate the information, keep in mind that people are less likely to take action if they have to work hard to understand what the data is telling them. It's therefore vital that insights are presented in a clear, concise and interesting way – this ensures the critical messages are understood and there's no room for misinterpretation.

You might be wondering why you need to think about disseminating information at such an early stage. The reason is your method(s) for presenting data may influence your data infrastructure requirements. Which leads us to…

5. *What are the infrastructure implications?*

Having defined what data is needed, how it will be turned into value, and how it will be communicated, the logical next step is working out the infrastructure implications of these decisions. Essentially this comes down to what software and hardware you'll need in order to capture, store, analyse and communicate insights from the data you have identified.

For example, if you're looking at gathering significantly more performance data, is your current data storage technology up to the task of storing all that new data, or do you need to supplement it with other solutions? What current analytic and reporting capabilities do you have and what else do you need to access?

We'll talk more about technology and infrastructure in Chapter 14 but, again, you will need to involve your in-house experts or an external data consultant.

6. *What action needs to be taken?*

Having answered the five questions above, you're now ready to define an action plan that turns your HR data strategy into reality. Like any action plan, this will include key milestones, actions and owners of those actions.

As part of this step, you will also need to identify training and development needs to help you put this plan into action, and pinpoint where you might need external help.

Making the business case for data- and AI-driven HR

There's no doubt that getting the leadership team and key decision makers involved will help you create a more robust data strategy. Not only that, getting leadership's buy-in at this crucial early stage means they're more likely to put your people-related data to good use in their own decision making.

Thus, an important part of creating a robust data strategy is making a strong business case for a data-driven HR approach, to help get people (both inside and outside the team) on board with the idea of data-driven HR. The more people are aware of and excited by the possibilities of data and AI, the more likely they are to buy into the idea.

This extends across all levels of the company and all functions, not just the company leadership. After all, data-driven HR is about people – and their data. When the people in an organization understand what data-driven HR is all about, and how it benefits the company as a whole and them as employees, they're more likely to be on board with, for example, capturing new kinds of employee data. When the business case for data-driven HR isn't communicated properly at every level, it can breed mistrust and have serious negative consequences on the organization's culture.

Making a business case for data-driven HR is a bit like an entrepreneur making a business case (or business plan) for their new venture. So, naturally, you'll want to do the same sorts of things as an entrepreneur would in their business plan. This includes giving a good outline of the data strategy and its goals (i.e. what you're hoping to achieve with data), as well as the tangible benefits to the business and its employees. It's also vital you're open and realistic about the timeframe, likely disruption to the business and costs, especially in discussions with the leadership team. You need to make the best case for data-driven HR, which means it's important not to gloss over these issues.

'Selling' data-driven HR is a crucial consideration on the way to intelligent HR. It instils confidence in data, inspires feelings of trust and transparency and emphasizes the HR team's value to the company as it works to achieve its goals. Plus, when you want your HR data to be used by other functions across the company, ensuring everyone understands the value of your people-related data means they're much more likely to incorporate that data into their decision making further down the line. By making a business case now, you're sowing the seeds for data-driven decision making and adding value through data in the future.

How you communicate your plan for data-driven HR depends on a number of factors, like how big your company is and the usual process for kicking off new initiatives. One good way to go about it is by distilling your data strategy into key points that can be communicated in a short presentation. Keep it simple and brief (there's no need to go into masses of detail on analytic possibilities, for instance) and remember that your enthusiasm for this new age of data-driven intelligent HR will be infectious. Use examples to demonstrate how other companies are leading the way in data-driven HR (you'll find plenty of these in Part Two). And remember to focus on the benefits that data-driven HR will bring, both to the organization as a whole and the people who work there.

Returning to your strategy in the future

No strategy is ever set in stone. Things change, markets shift, organizational priorities evolve, and so on. It's therefore very likely that you will need to revisit your data strategy on a regular basis (annually, at least) to check it's still in line with the company's overall priorities. Even if nothing has changed, revisiting the strategy helps you to stay lean and remain focused on your desired outcomes.

Also keep in mind that, as you get further down the road of data-driven HR, significant new opportunities or questions may present themselves. For example, when answering one of your strategic questions, the data may throw up other, more pressing questions that also need to be answered, and this may lead to a slight tweak in your strategy. The technology around data and analytics is evolving fast and what's possible in one or two years' time may be completely different from what's possible now. While you want to follow through on the actions in your strategy, remember that the point of data-driven HR is to add greater value to the organization and do things in a more intelligent, streamlined way. It therefore makes sense to stay alert to new ways of doing that.

Key takeaways

Let's finish up with a quick recap on strategy:

- It's vital you have a strategy that maps out how HR will use data and AI to help drive the business forward. Having such a strategy in place ensures you stay focused on your goals and target your resources most effectively.

- There are three main ways data and AI can add value to the work that HR teams do: generating better insights, providing a better service to employees and driving efficiencies in HR.

- Any good strategy starts with your objectives. What are your biggest people-related challenges or most pressing HR goals? When identifying your objectives, ensure they link to the organization's overarching strategic goals. And do try to keep your list of objectives to just a few key goals.

- With your objectives in mind, you can now begin to create your data strategy, using the six key questions outlined in this chapter. It's really important you have wider buy-in for your data strategy, so be sure to involve key stakeholders – including leadership and the IT function. If you do not have in-house data/IT expertise, a data consultant will be able to help you develop your strategy.

- Finally, don't forget to revisit your strategy on a regular basis to check it's still in line with the company's overall priorities. Revisiting the strategy also helps you remain focused on your desired outcomes.

As we've seen in this chapter, generating better insights is one of the most impactful ways HR teams can use data and AI. So let's delve into this topic in more detail and see how the HR function can deploy data and AI tools to improve decision making.

Notes

1 M McNeill. How 5 successful companies are using HR analytics, ICS Learn, 17 May 2020. www.icslearn.co.uk/blog/human-resources/how-5-successful-companies-are-using-hr-analytics (archived at https://perma.cc/6LNJ-799Y)

2 Business Insurance. Walmart using AI tools to help staff find right medical provider, Business Insurance, 1 February 2022. www.businessinsurance.com/article/20220201/STORY/912347597/Walmart-using-AI-tools-to-help-staff-find-right-medical-provider (archived at https://perma.cc/GG5P-ZB3M)

3 A M Klahre. 3 ways Johnson & Johnson is taking talent acquisition to the next level, Johnson & Johnson, 29 August 2017. www.jnj.com/innovation/3-ways-johnson-and-johnson-is-taking-talent-acquisition-to-the-next-level (archived at https://perma.cc/NRW2-4PQ6)

PART TWO
Data-driven and AI-enabled HR in practice

Now that we've laid the groundwork for intelligent HR, let's look at practical uses of data and AI. Each chapter in Part Two will focus on a specific area of HR, setting out ways in which data and AI can optimize HR processes, drive performance, and contribute to the organization's success. Throughout, we'll explore real-world examples of how organizations have deployed data and AI to great success.

Better HR insights and decision making 06

As we saw in Chapter 5, delivering people-related insights and aiding decision making are two of HR's core functions. With data and AI-enabled tools, HR teams can generate better insights than ever before and improve people-related decision making across the organization. By analysing large datasets and applying advanced AI algorithms, HR teams can identify trends and patterns in key HR metrics such as turnover, employee engagement and performance – allowing them to develop more informed and data-driven strategies for recruitment, retention, performance and development. The work of HR becomes more strategic and forward-thinking – to the extent that you can even create early warning systems capable of identifying potential workforce issues before they become critical. Such early warning systems can enable you to take proactive action to mitigate risks and optimize workforce performance.

By leveraging data and AI in this way, HR teams can become more agile, responsive and strategic, while at the same time creating a more human-centric approach to workforce management. And as an added bonus, these tools can also make compliance reporting much less cumbersome.

This all comes under the topic of *HR analytics*. Needless to say I could write a whole book on HR analytics alone, so consider this chapter an overview of how HR analytics can give your organization better insights.

The role of HR analytics

HR analytics is, as the name suggests, the process of gathering and analysing HR data to provide useful insights, improve decision making and boost workplace performance. You might also be familiar with the terms *people analytics*, *talent analytics* and *workforce analytics* – it's all the same thing.

What's involved?

HR analytics breaks down into a few different steps. In the first instance the data is collected (and this can be internal or external data). Then the data is analysed using statistical models and machine learning techniques to identify patterns and trends (this may involve comparing the data against other data, such as benchmarks or historical information). And then the insights gained from that process are used to inform decision making.

It's really important that this whole process builds on your HR data strategy (Chapter 5) – by which I mean the data that you collect and analyse must help the HR function achieve its core goals and contribute to the organization's strategic objectives. Of course, HR analytics also provides a way for the HR team to measure and demonstrate how it contributes to the organization's performance. Win–win.

Why do we need HR analytics?

Because it's how we turn *data* into *insights*. And as we've already seen in this book, data in and of itself isn't enough to enable key decision makers to take action. You need HR analytics to pull out the meaning within the data. You need HR analytics to identify trends and patterns within your data – which can, in turn, help you predict upcoming issues. And you need HR analytics to answer your most pressing questions. Questions such as 'Which of our employees are most likely to leave in the next 12 months?', 'What are the best indicators of success in candidates?' and 'How does our development programme impact employee satisfaction and performance?' HR analytics takes the guesswork out of answering these questions so that you can decide on the best way forward.

In short, HR analytics enables more accurate decision making, both within the HR function and for managers and leaders across the business. That said, HR analytics isn't without its pitfalls. You need good-quality data (data that is free from bias, etc. – see Chapter 4). You may have multiple existing management and reporting systems to deal with, which can make it difficult to pull data together (more on technology and infrastructure in Chapter 14). You need to invest in the AI tools to analyse that data, whether that means creating in-house analytics systems or purchasing off-the-shelf HR analytics tools. And you need to ensure that these technologies are used ethically, transparently and with the proper oversight (again, see Chapter 4). These are not insignificant issues but, as we'll see in this chapter, HR analytics can deliver huge rewards.

HR analytics in action

Take German energy company E.ON as an example. When employee absenteeism rose above benchmark, E.ON's HR team deployed HR analytics to figure out which factors were driving unscheduled time off. One theory was that employees selling holiday days back to the company increased absenteeism, but it turned out that wasn't the case. Instead, analytics uncovered that the duration and timing of vacation had the biggest impact on absenteeism – as in, people who took multiple days off across the year and had at least one longer vacation took less unscheduled time off.[1] As a result, employees were encouraged to take frequent short breaks and at least one longer break across the year – and managers were encouraged to be more accommodating when it came to approving time off. If the HR team had simply acted on gut instinct and stopped the practice of employees selling back holiday – which was not proven to have any statistical impact on absenteeism – it likely would have been an unpopular and ineffective decision.

The evolution of HR analytics

In Chapter 2 we saw how the work of HR has evolved, and how data has come to play a more vital role in HR. Now let's explore how HR analytics has evolved significantly over the past few decades. Driven by new technologies, data availability and increasing recognition of the strategic value of HR in organizations, HR analytics has evolved from basic data reporting and descriptive analysis to more sophisticated analytics, incorporating AI and machine learning technologies.

From the pre-analytics era to descriptive and diagnostic analytics

Before the advent of HR analytics, HR decision making was largely based on a mixture of gut feeling and experience. In terms of data, HR professionals relied on traditional sources like annual performance reviews, exit interviews and employee surveys to inform their decisions.

As HR analytics began to evolve, systems largely focused on *descriptive analytics*, which involved gathering and presenting data on employee demographics, retention rates, turnover and other fundamental HR metrics. This stage was marked by the emergence of HR information systems and management systems that helped organizations store and manage employee data more effectively.

Then, as HR analytics matured, *diagnostic analytics* emerged, enabling HR professionals to identify patterns and relationships in their data. This phase involved the use of data visualization tools and basic statistical analysis techniques to explore the causes of specific HR issues, such as high turnover or low employee engagement.

The move towards predictive and prescriptive analytics

With advancements in technology and the increasing availability of data, HR analytics has increasingly shifted towards *predictive analytics*. This involves applying advanced statistical models and machine learning techniques to historical data in order to forecast future outcomes (such as employee turnover, performance, recruitment success, and so on). This leap forward in analytics has allowed organizations to make more informed decisions by anticipating potential challenges and identifying opportunities for improvement. In other words, the emphasis has shifted somewhat from solving current and past problems to predicting future problems and solving them before they occur.

The most recent stage in the evolution of HR analytics is *prescriptive analytics*, which goes beyond simply predicting outcomes to recommending specific actions. By incorporating optimization algorithms and decision analysis, prescriptive analytics enables HR professionals to identify the best course of action for a given situation, such as talent development, workforce planning or employee engagement initiatives.

In one example, Microsoft used HR analytics to develop statistical profiles of employees who are most at risk of leaving their jobs. Based on these insights, the HR team could enact a variety of interventions, such as discussing learning opportunities or assigning a mentor. With this approach, Microsoft's HR team was able to cut attrition rates in high turnover parts of the business by more than half.[2]

Clearly, the integration of AI into HR analytics has significantly expanded its capabilities. Advanced algorithms can analyse vast amounts of data, uncover hidden patterns and generate insights that were previously unattainable. As a result, HR professionals and executives can make more informed decisions, identify trends, and develop more tailored interventions for individual employees or teams.

So, what can be measured and analysed with HR analytics?

Pretty much anything to do with the workforce. Essentially, you're looking for metrics that help you understand what's working well at the moment, where you might have room for improvement, and what trends and issues may be coming up on the horizon.

The following aren't exhaustive lists by any means, but they indicate some of the metrics that are commonly used in HR analytics. Which metrics are right for you? Largely this will be informed by your HR data strategy (Chapter 5). But you will also need to talk to decision makers across the organization to determine which metrics they need most in order to make better decisions. We'll talk more about getting information to decision makers later in the chapter.

Example recruitment metrics

- cost per hire
- time to hire
- acceptance rate
- new hire turnover (typically, employees who leave within the first year)
- time to productivity

Using metrics like these you can, for example, understand how long it takes to hire for specific roles, which in turn allows managers to better plan their hiring. And with advanced tools, it's even possible to scan your organization's entire employment history to determine the key attributes for a particular position. That's the idea behind Watson Recruitment, an AI tool by IBM. Watson can also be used to scan applicants to find the most appropriate candidates based on desired attributes.[3]

How are companies using recruitment metrics in practice? One example comes from media information company Nielsen. Using HR analytics, the team determined that the first year of employment played a critical role in how likely an employee was to stick around. Based on this knowledge, Nielsen implemented a system to ensure that critical contact points for first-year employees were met. For example, if the first check-in with their manager didn't happen within a set timeframe – an important condition for new hire retention – it triggered a notification.

Elsewhere, Johnson & Johnson used HR analytics to analyse the impact of industry experience on new hire retention. Previously, recruiters had assumed that those with industry experience would be more likely to stay with the company and be quicker to contribute to company performance, as opposed to people who were fresh out of college. But the data actually revealed that employees hired straight out of college remained with the organization significantly longer than more experienced candidates – and there was no real difference in how quickly they contributed to performance. As a result, the company increased hires of recent graduates by 20 per cent.

Example performance metrics

- employee performance
- performance and potential
- goal tracking
- capability analytics (identifying core competencies in the workforce)
- capacity analytics (operational efficiency of employees)
- leadership performance

With metrics like these, you can better grasp employee, team and organizational performance – identifying, for example, which employees are star performers and which attributes top performers have in common. This knowledge can inform future hiring decisions, as well.

In one example, a mining company in Zimbabwe was concerned about losing money as a result of understaffed or overstaffed departments. To identify optimum staffing levels, they measured the number of employees in a business unit and compared that to the business unit's activity over 17 quarters. They found a strong relationship between business activity and number of employees, and this helped them identify which departments were understaffed and which were overstaffed. Employees from overstaffed units were either retrenched or relocated to understaffed departments, and within three months the company was saving money.[4]

Example employee retention and satisfaction metrics

- employee engagement score (for example, using the employee net promoter score)
- retention rate

- turnover rate/employee churn
- absenteeism

Using metrics like these, you can identify trends in retention, predict which employees might be at risk of leaving, and develop strategies to better engage with those employees.

You can also explore the relationship between engagement and performance, which is what shoe retailer Clarks did. By analysing 450 data points, the company was able to confirm that high engagement does indeed lead to higher business performance, with each 1 per cent of improvement in engagement delivering a 0.4 per cent improvement in business performance. The team also analysed the characteristics of the 100 top-performing stores and one of the things they found was that a longer tenure of the store manager was a significant predictor of store performance. So switching store managers on a regular basis was a no-no for team engagement and performance.

Example training and development metrics

- cost of training per employee
- training effectiveness
- training completion rate
- time to completion
- time since last promotion

Using training and development metrics, you can better understand how employees engage with your training offering, identify areas for improvement and find out which employees may be overdue for development. In one example, International Scholarship and Tuition Services used HR analytics to better spot potential development opportunities, which meant they were able to ensure the right employees got on track for leadership roles.

Using HR analytics to inform decision making: Reporting and dashboards

Much of the time, HR analytics will be relevant to, well, the HR team! But that's not exclusively the case. Because decision makers across the business will also need access to the insights you uncover. In this final part of the chapter, let's dwell on the process of turning insights into decisions and actions – both within HR and across the business.

Reporting to others in the business

For me, intelligent, data-driven HR is about HR becoming the strategic partner for the organization – by which I mean providing leaders and managers with key insights about people, developing early warning systems, and generally preparing the organization for the future. Because the nature of work is changing fast, and what it takes to gain competitive advantage is fast evolving. The HR function will play a vital role in making sure the organization is in the best position for success (a great example being building future skills and identifying skills gaps – see Chapters 10 and 13).

But to achieve this vision of HR as the company's strategic partner, you need to be able to communicate insights to those who need them most. The good news is that most HR analytics tools make reporting easier than ever, but here are a few overarching tips on reporting insights:

Reporting insights

- *Identify the audience for each metric:* Some metrics will be exclusively for the HR team, some may be relevant to middle managers, while others are needed by the executive team. By identifying the right audience, you can avoid reporting metrics to people who really don't need them and ensure reports are always relevant. With this in mind...

- *Ask decision makers what information they need:* What are their reporting needs? What information are they currently not getting? What information are they getting that they currently don't use? Which leads me to...

- *Revisit your HR analytics frequently to ensure they're actually useful:* For example, if you commonly report on data that it later turns out isn't helpful for decision makers (in HR and elsewhere), then you may want to adjust your reporting accordingly. Remember, data should lead to insights which lead to action. If data doesn't lead to action, do you really need to keep measuring that metric?

Of course, sometimes you may need to deploy HR analytics for more ad hoc projects, as opposed to regular reporting. Say your organization wants to open an office in a new location but isn't sure of the right location. In that case, the HR team can contribute significant value to the decision-making process.

That's exactly what happened at technology multinational Cisco. When the company wanted to open a new regional office in California, they turned to HR analytics to pinpoint the best location and even the right building. The goal was to identify the best spot according to a number of factors, but especially the ability to attract talent in that location. The People Planning Analytics and Tools team sourced data such as office usage rates and costs, and availability of talent (specifically from neighbouring universities). Interestingly, the data ended up pointing Cisco leaders to a different location than one they originally had in mind, because the data indicated it would have been more difficult to attract talent in that area. Now, Cisco's process for selecting and opening new offices routinely involves people analytics.

Using HR dashboards

HR dashboards are a great way to analyse and communicate data, and aid decision making. Think of the dashboard as a tool that pulls all the HR metrics together in one place, summarizes information, identifies insights and turns those insights into easy-to-digest reports and visualizations. Basically, the HR dashboard is a decision-making tool both for HR and the wider organization.

There are many different types of HR dashboards available – many of them cloud-based and incorporating AI techniques, with some that specialize in specific areas (such as recruitment or performance). They're typically very user-friendly, highly customizable, and regularly updated with new features. Well-known examples include BambooHR, Personio, QuestionPro and Bob.

Key takeaways

To recap the main points on HR analytics:

- With HR analytics, HR teams can generate better insights than ever before, which enables the organization to make more accurate people-related decisions.

- As HR analytics has evolved from descriptive analytics to predictive and prescriptive analytics, this has allowed the work of HR to become more strategic and forward-thinking – to the extent that you can even create early warning systems capable of identifying potential workforce issues before they become critical.

- Pretty much anything people-related can be measured with HR analytics, including recruitment and retention, performance, training and development, employee engagement and more.

- The right metrics for you will largely depend on your HR data strategy. But, essentially, you're looking for metrics that help you understand what's working well, where you might have room for improvement and what trends and issues may be coming up on the horizon.

- HR analytics platforms make reporting to decision makers (within HR and across the organization) easier than ever. Remember, data-driven HR is about HR becoming the strategic partner for the organization – by providing leaders and managers with key insights about people, developing early warning systems and generally preparing the organization for the future. HR dashboards and other reporting tools will help you get the information to those who need it most.

It's clear that data and AI can drastically improve the decision-making process in HR activities, including recruitment. But how else can data and AI enhance the recruitment and selection process? Turn to the next chapter to find out.

Notes

1 M Ankum. People analytics: 5 real case studies, Effectory, 4 March 2022. www. effectory.com/knowledge/people-analytics-5-real-case-studies (archived at https://perma.cc/67KP-T4XK)

2 M McNeill. How 5 successful companies are using HR analytics, ICS Learn. 17 May 2020. www.icslearn.co.uk/blog/human-resources/how-5-successful-companies-are-using-hr-analytics (archived at https://perma.cc/XJY6-8PAN)

3 HR 360. Here's how IBM is using artificial intelligence to help boost their human resource capabilities, HR 360, 2021. hr360.wbresearch.com/blog/ibm-watson-ai-for-hr-recruit-reskill (archived at https://perma.cc/6V7N-DZGF)

4 T Fica. The 29 most important HR metrics you need to track examples of how companies use HR analytics, BambooHR, 2 February 2023. www.bamboohr.com/blog/key-hr-metrics#examples-of-how-companies-use-hr-analytics (archived at https://perma.cc/3WFZ-78YE)

Recruitment and candidate selection

07

AI and data are increasingly being used in recruitment and selection to optimize the hiring process – and I firmly believe that those HR teams who embrace data and AI are the ones who will recruit most successfully in the coming years. Why exactly? Because AI algorithms can identify patterns in large datasets and extract valuable insights that help HR professionals to better match job candidates with the requirements of the role, improve the candidate experience and reduce bias in the hiring process. Plus, as we'll see in this chapter, automation is helping to streamline intelligent recruitment by automating aspects of candidate assessment and selection.

In this chapter we'll explore some of the main ways in which data and AI can help to enhance your recruitment activities. Broadly speaking, they are: boosting your employer brand; identifying the best recruitment channels; identifying and assessing the most suitable candidates; and streamlining recruitment with AI-enhanced automation tools.

Boosting your employer brand

As any marketing colleague will tell you, branding is absolutely vital when it comes to attracting and retaining customers (in this case, employees). What's more, your employer brand should ideally align with your overall company, service or product brand. If the two are sending different messages – ethical manufacturer with questionable employee ethics, for example – you could struggle to attract the best talent. One paper by Randstad RiseSmart stated that nearly 70 per cent of unemployed job seekers would not take a job with an employer who had an iffy reputation.[1] On the flip side, the same paper stated that 84 per cent of employees would consider jacking in their current job to move to an employer with an excellent reputation, even if the salary increase was less than 10 per cent.

Using data to monitor your brand

Your employer brand tells employees and potential employees who you are as a company, what you stand for, what it's like to be part of the company and what makes you different from other employers. When developing your employer brand, you'll want to consider what kind of talent you want to attract; or, to put it another way, what kind of people best fit with your company's culture and goals.

Having identified this, you need to be sure this brand image chimes with reality. And this is where data and AI algorithms come into play. You should look to test your employment brand at regular intervals. Sentiment analysis of interview and survey responses, as well social media posts, can really help establish how successful your employer brand is. And if your company goes through major changes, such as a restructuring, you should absolutely look to assess the impact of this change on your brand. Measuring sentiment before, during and after the changes will give vital insights that will help you manage the transition and maintain a positive employer brand.

No doubt you've heard of the employer net promoter score. Indeed, these days, 'How likely are you to recommend the company?' is a common question on employee surveys. However, rather than take the temperature of this once a year, many companies are using anonymous 'pulse' surveys, asking just this one simple question on a weekly, monthly or quarterly basis.

Creating and maintaining a positive employer brand is not just about keeping your current employees happy; it's also about how attractive your company appears to outsiders. What factors do you think attract potential employees to your company or make an employee more likely to recommend you as an employer? Salary? Flexible working? No and no, according to data. Josh Bersin's company analysed Glassdoor data from more than 6,000 companies and 2.2 million employees to get some interesting findings on employer brand.[2] It turned out the biggest factor in whether employees would recommend their company as a place to work was 'culture and values'. In fact, an employee's rating on culture and values is almost five times more predictive of a company being recommended than salary and benefits. Among those under the age of 35, 'career opportunities' was the top driver of employer brand. This demonstrates the need for employers to consider culture and employee development as much as, or even more than, the usual salary and benefits.

I'm not saying decent salaries and benefits don't impact employer brand, but it's clear that people want to feel truly at home in a company. They want to enjoy the culture, they want to be proud of the company they work for, and they want their input to be valued through good development opportunities. These are all elements to focus on when it comes to boosting your employer brand and promoting that brand outside the organization.

Immersing potential employees in your employer brand

Another key element of branding is of course raising the profile of your employer brand among potential employees. This is especially worthwhile if you're in a highly competitive industry, like the tech world, where you're struggling to attract talent. Some innovative organizations are using data-related technology like virtual reality to capitalize on this idea, delivering 360-degree videos that show people what it's really like to work at the company. This helps employers show off their culture, give an authentic feel for everyday life within the business and attract the best candidates.

One of my favourite examples comes from the unlikely world of US college football. The University of Minnesota's Golden Gophers team created a slick VR experience to help sign up in-demand players. Described as a 'day in the life of a Golden Gopher', the VR experience serves to immerse candidates and tell a compelling story about what it's really like to be part of the team – with footage of practices, games, workouts, those all-important UM campus experiences, city life and even the Minnesota weather. In the competitive world of college football it can be hard to stand out and convey the benefits of signing with a smaller team. VR is a great way to do this authentically.

Taking the idea of immersive VR experiences to the next level, some organizations are now using the metaverse to show off their employer brand and attract candidates. French retail group Carrefour, for example, held a virtual recruitment session in the metaverse.[3] For a retail company with huge digital ambitions, the event appeared to be designed to attract those with digital skills and to promote Carrefour as an innovative employer – in other words, to help the company stand out in a field where competition for digital skills is intense. For many organizations, showing up in the metaverse will be a key way to attract talent and demonstrate their appeal as an employer. From a marketing perspective – which is, after all, what employer branding is all about – the metaverse makes a lot of sense. But we'll talk more about the metaverse later in the chapter.

Identifying the most effective recruitment channels for you

Most companies use a mix of recruitment channels, including headhunters, job forums, social media campaigns and LinkedIn searches. Different channels work better for different industries, or even different positions within the same company. Given the diversity of recruitment channels, it's important to know which deliver the greatest return on investment. In my work with clients, I'd estimate that maybe 50 per cent of recruitment spend is wasted. If a channel isn't driving actual recruitment, you should stop recruiting through that channel immediately and focus on those channels that deliver the most value for your spend.

Understanding more about your recruitment channels

The beauty of data is that it allows you to test your recruitment channels and measure their success rate. These days, it's possible to measure everything minutely. So, rather than focus on obvious indicators like how many resumes you get in response from different channels (which only tells you volume, not quality), you could look instead at more valuable indicators like how many offers were made to candidates from particular channels. You could even take this further and assess your most successful employees in particular roles and pinpoint which channels they came from. Many of today's HR analytics platforms (see Chapter 6) can help you assess this and more, so that you can target your recruitment appropriately.

A good example of this comes from Marriott Hotels. The hospitality giant has a popular recruitment page on Facebook with, at the time of writing, more than 1.3 million likes and high volumes of people engaging with the page on a daily and weekly basis. The page obviously lists available jobs, but it also beautifully demonstrates what it's like to work for the chain through photos and videos of life behind the scenes in the hotels. It makes sense that a hospitality business like Marriott wants to attract the classic 'people person', which explains why social media is such a useful recruitment channel for Marriott. It's an excellent lesson for any company looking to maximize their employment channels – go with the channel most used by the type of people you want to attract. To build on their Facebook success, Marriott even created a Facebook game called MyMarriottHotel, where potential employees could learn how to manage hotels.

Experimenting with not-so-obvious recruitment channels

Sometimes, though, you may need to think a little further outside the recruitment box and look for entirely new channels to recruit talent – particularly in areas where there's a lot of competition to hire the best talent. Data scientists are one such group that are in great demand at all kinds of businesses, yet there just aren't enough people with the required skills. To overcome this problem, Walmart decided to get creative. Rather than advertise through traditional channels, they turned to crowdsourced analytics competition platform Kaggle to find the talent they needed. At Kaggle, an army of 'armchair data scientists' apply their skills to analytical problems submitted by companies, with the designer of the best solution being rewarded – in this case with a job at Walmart.

Candidates were provided with a set of historical sales data from a sample of stores, along with associated sales events, such as clearance sales and price rollbacks. They were asked to come up with models showing how these events would affect sales across a number of departments. As a result of the competition, several people were hired into the analytics team.[4] Interestingly, the crowdsourced approach led to some appointments of people who, ordinarily, wouldn't have been considered for an interview based on their resumes alone. One candidate, for example, had a very strong background in physics but no formal analytics background.

While you may not be looking to recruit an army of data scientists like Walmart, this example shows why it's important to consider some of the more unusual recruitment channels, find out where your talent hangs out and use that knowledge to focus on recruitment channels that deliver the most bang for your buck.

Identifying and assessing the best candidates for your business

I've often heard that recruiters and hiring managers make up their minds whether or not to hire a prospective candidate within five minutes of sitting down with them. It's hard to say whether this is true or not, but many HR professionals or hiring managers would probably admit that they had made appointments based on a gut feeling – simply whether or not they felt the person was the right fit for the role.

As it is in many other areas of business, data and analytics is helping to take the guesswork out of recruitment. Rather than relying on the famous gut feeling, those teams taking a data- and AI-enabled approach are finding it leads to more suitable hires who stay happy and on the job for longer. In my opinion, this is where the future of recruitment lies.

Predicting a candidate's suitability

When recruiting a new candidate, you're not just looking at a list of skills and experience on paper. Personality and fit are just as important. Traditionally, these factors have been considered difficult to judge, but not with the help of data and predictive analytics...

We already know that companies like Facebook and Google can predict an awful lot about our intelligence, behaviour and personality attributes based on our profiles and online activities. A study by researchers at Cambridge University and Microsoft Research Labs showed how the patterns of Facebook likes can be used to automatically predict a range of highly sensitive personal attributes.[5] For example, likes for curly fries, science, Mozart, thunderstorms or *The Daily Show* predicted high intelligence, while likes for Harley Davidson, Lady Antebellum, and 'I love being a mom' predicted low intelligence. The study was even able to predict sexuality and religion with extraordinary accuracy.

Creepy? A little. But the same sort of predictive capabilities can be put to good use when it comes to identifying the right employees. It sounds obvious, but the first step is to identify exactly what you're looking for. JetBlue Airlines gives us a great example of this. Originally, the company had focused on 'niceness' as the most important attribute for its flight attendants. Then, after carrying out some customer data analysis with the Wharton Business School, the company was interested to find that, in the eyes of their customers, being helpful is actually more important than being nice – and can even make up for people being not so nice. The company was then able to use this information to narrow down candidates more effectively.[6]

What does your ideal employee look like, in terms of skills, desirable attributes, personality traits, qualifications, experience and fit? Armed with this 'shopping list', if you like, it's relatively easy to use AI tools to sift through potential candidates and identify certain data points in applications, resumes or profiles and find the candidates with the best fit.

While the final hiring decision should always come down to a human, AI tools can save a lot of time by narrowing the field down from maybe hundreds of candidates to the most suitable 10 or 20. Clearly, then, this is one area where AI-driven automation is playing an increasingly important role. We'll talk more about automation a little later in the chapter, but suffice to say that AI tools are helping employers filter out much of the 'noise' when it comes to narrowing down candidates and focusing on what they really want. Crucially, such automation can also remove the biases that humans inevitably bring to the recruitment process. But, again, we'll get to that later.

CASE STUDY Identifying candidates for top-level positions

Data and analytics can be used to identify the best candidates for any position, even right up to the 'C-suite' of executives who guide the direction of the business. These leaders carry a large amount of responsibility, and in return often take home a sizeable chunk of a business's earnings. When mistakes are made appointing people at this level, it can spell disaster. So, of course, it makes sense that filling these vacancies should be done with as little guesswork as possible.

Corporate headhunters Korn Ferry have taken steps to ensure C-level recruitment is firmly rooted in data and analytics. Thanks to the wealth of data collected in the company's long history, they were able to draw up detailed profiles of the competencies, traits and experiences needed to succeed at the top level. The data revealed some strong patterns about the important traits and qualities required for C-level positions, including being a lifelong learner, higher levels of emotional intelligence and empathy, communication skills and a tolerance for risk.[7]

In partnership with data scientists at the University of Southern California, Korn Ferry built an analytics-based people placement platform called Four Dimensional Executive Assessment – or KF4D for short – which can assess traits and competencies, experience and even cultural fit. When it comes to the latter, clients looking to fill positions have the ability to choose whether they're happy with their organizational culture, in which case the system will find someone who is likely to fit in. Or, if they're looking to change their culture, candidates will be suggested who are likely to be agents of change.

Appointing a new CEO is undoubtedly one of the biggest challenges a business will ever face. Most companies wouldn't make decisions about which products or services to offer without solid data analysis, so it makes sense to bring the same analytical approach to hiring for top-level positions.

Sourcing freelancers and remote workers

In this connected world, it's now increasingly common for companies to draw upon remote talent without making traditional hires. As more and more businesses head for the cloud, it's becoming much easier for companies to tap into gig economy talent. The obvious advantage for workers is they can work whenever and wherever they like. And for employers, they can benefit from talent without the expense of hiring people full time.

And even when companies do want to hire full-time talent, more and more are letting employees work remotely – particularly since the pandemic. But what does this mean for recruitment? Well, the same sorts of analytic techniques we've talked about in this chapter can be incredibly useful when identifying and assessing candidates who may never set foot in your offices. Also, when someone works remotely, they may not have access to the same level of one-to-one mentorship that an in-house employee may have. This may mean you need to focus your hiring on highly experienced people who already have all the core attributes needed to succeed in the role. Data and analytics can help you pinpoint such candidates quickly and easily – and ensure you onboard remote workers successfully (more about onboarding in Chapter 8).

Identifying and promoting suitable candidates inside the company

As a final word on identifying candidates, many employers see it as more cost-effective to promote from within than to recruit from outside the company. Another obvious advantage of internal candidates is they're already well versed in the company's systems, processes and culture. So it makes sense to apply the same sort of talent analytics to identifying suitable candidates from within the company. We already know that the opportunity to progress and grow within a company is hugely attractive to employees, so promoting from within is another great way to boost your employer brand.

As we saw in Chapter 6, people analytics can help HR teams identify the top performers in roles across the company, as well as those who are already in the best position for them.

AI-enhanced automation in recruitment

As we've already seen in this chapter, AI and data are increasingly being used by HR functions to automate and, in turn, streamline parts of the recruitment and selection process. So let's dwell on this notion a little deeper, and see what can be automated – and where companies may fall foul of automation.

What can be automated?

When it comes to recruitment, how do you, an HR professional, add the most value for the organization and people you serve? I'd bet your answers include making decisions based on your expertise and perspective, identifying and plugging skills gaps, finding the very best talent, convincing sought-after candidates to come work for your employer, improving your organization's employer brand and generally providing an awesome service to internal and external candidates. And yet how much of your (or your team members') time is really spent on those mission-critical tasks? How much of your team's time is spent on mechanical, easily automated tasks like scheduling interviews, answering basic questions or sifting through the many irrelevant applications that come your way?

This is where automation can provide massive advantages for the average HR team – taking care of the easily repeatable tasks and freeing up recruiters' time for more value-adding activities. In particular, the combination of *robotic process automation* – software that automates business processes that are rules-based, structured and repetitive – with machine learning is where a lot of value lies. The robotic process automation takes care of repetitive tasks, while the AI element can enhance and speed up decision making.

There are many recruitment automation platforms out there that combine robotic process automation and AI elements, often referred to as *applicant tracking systems.* Here are some of the recruitment and selection tasks that they promise to automate:

- You can automate the creation and posting of job adverts, according to templates that you set. That way, you don't have to reformat or rewrite the same posting for different sites and manually upload them to dozens or even hundreds of boards – the system will automatically populate multiple boards, based on your job description and typical ad template. Some tools are even capable of identifying the target audience for specific job posts and automatically buying ad space (within a defined budget) that's optimal for that audience.

- You can automatically pre-screen candidates according to must-have credentials, from professional certifications to the legal right to live and work in your part of the world. This ensures recruiters don't waste time on non-eligible candidates. But you can also take pre-screening further, by adding questions to the application process that can be scored and ranked according to desirability. This allows your recruiters to hone in on the best (on paper) candidates first, potentially speeding up your time to hire.

- You can also automate some candidate assessments, such as cognitive testing or personality questionnaires. The system will then assess and rank the candidates. In one example, IBM used AI to identify the best candidates to join a sales team based on their social skills – with the system even predicting the impact those people would have on the sales team's performance. As new team members are added to the team, the AI tool continually re-assesses the skills needed with the aim of forming the optimum sales team.[8]

- You can even have the AI system automatically shortlist and contact the best candidates, thereby quickly securing them an interview – and automatically reject the least suitable candidates according to your pre-set criteria, thereby giving those candidates a fast resolution. However, automatically selecting and rejecting candidates without human oversight should be used with caution – see later in the chapter.

- You can also automate the sourcing of resumes and candidates. Basically, you create a list of requirements, and then the system will scour platforms looking for the most suitable profiles. This can extend to social media platforms as well – meaning the system can identify suitable candidates and send them tailored messages.

- You can use AI-powered chatbots to automate communication throughout the recruitment process – for example, answering candidates' common questions or sending them a progress update. This saves recruiters sending the same messages over and over again, and ensures consistency. And for the candidate, it helps to ensure they get quick responses and remain in the loop.

- You may also be able to automate due diligence checks, such as reference requests and background checks.

- You can even automate interview scheduling, which can be especially helpful when you're recruiting high volumes of candidates. Recruiters and hiring managers define their availability and then the candidate can choose the available slot that best suits them, so there's no back-and-forth between various parties.

- You can automate first-round interviews with one-way video interviewing, where the recruiter sets the questions in advance and then the candidates record their responses. Hilton has used digital interviewing platform HireVue to conduct one-way video interviews (for first-stage interviews) with multiple candidates at once. This helped the company quickly assess which candidates were the best fit, and which should therefore progress to the next interview stage – and in doing so, Hilton was able to reduce its time to hire from 43 days down to an impressive five days.[9]

- You can automate internal recruitment workflows – for example, prompting hiring managers to review a shortlist of candidates, or give their feedback for candidates. This can save masses of time for busy recruiters.

- You can also use predictive analytics to forecast workforce needs and identify potential skill gaps in your organization. This allows you to proactively develop talent pipelines and recruitment strategies.

- And don't forget, you can automate recruitment reporting. (Circle back to Chapter 6 on HR analytics.)

Clearly, automating tasks like these can help to free up recruiter time, improve recruiter productivity (by up to 50 per cent, according to recruitment automation specialists Entelo),[10] speed up time to hire (Entelo says by up to 15 per cent), reduce organizational costs (because positions are vacant for less time) and provide a slicker experience for candidates.

Automation in action

CASE STUDY   Johnson & Johnson

We've already seen a few quick examples of automation in action, but let's explore how Johnson & Johnson has automated one part of the recruitment process with great success – in this case, using Google's Cloud Talent Solution to better match people visiting J&J's career site with suitable job listings. This had been a problem for J&J in the past. While the company receives around one million applications for 25,000 jobs each year, the proportion of applicants that were highly qualified for those positions was low. Recruiters noticed that even when visitors to the site had a strong match for certain positions, those opportunities weren't displayed in search results. Candidates couldn't easily find the right job opportunities, and the system wasn't working. This is where Cloud Talent Solution comes in. By understanding the nuances of job seeker search queries and job postings, the system uses machine learning to help candidates find the jobs most relevant to them. This meant J&J recruiters didn't have to manually optimize job postings for search results, and job seekers could find jobs on the J&J site more easily. As a result, J&J has seen a 41 per cent increase in high-quality applicants per search, and a 45 per cent increase in click-through rate on its job site.[11]

For those recruiters concerned that they may find themselves out of a job thanks to automation software, I wouldn't lose too much sleep. We still have marketers and sales people, despite marketing and sales automation software existing for years. But it's fair to expect that the work of recruiters will shift and evolve – moving away from repetitive tasks and spending more time on the tasks that drive the business forward. Which sounds great. However, it's vitally important to ensure that these automation technologies are used ethically and transparently, and that human oversight is maintained. If we abdicate all responsibility for hiring decisions to machines, this can result in unintended consequences and unfair outcomes. As some organizations have discovered to their detriment...

The downsides of automation

Perhaps the best-known example of automated recruitment gone wrong comes from Amazon. As we saw in Chapter 4, the company had to stop using a machine learning algorithm for screening candidates because it was biased against female candidates. So what happened? In essence, the data the algorithm used to make decisions was flawed because Amazon's recruitment data from the previous 10 years included more male than female candidates (historically, more men had applied for roles). As such, the system effectively taught itself that male candidates were preferable to female.[12] The system was so skewed, it penalized resumes that included the word 'women'.

Amazon made a couple of big mistakes with its system. For one thing, the data used was purely internal – and even in a company as big as Amazon, there clearly wasn't enough data to ensure diversity and fairness. Synthetic data would have helped to solve this issue. And secondly, as with any aspect of business, it's not always a great idea to base future decisions on what you've done in the past. Just because certain candidates have traditionally done well in the hiring process doesn't mean that's the best outcome for the business going forward. Remember, Amazon was using recruitment data from the previous 10 years and *a lot* can change in 10 years.

Interestingly, at the time of writing, leaked Amazon documents suggest that the company has again been experimenting with software to screen its job applicants – and is preparing, reports suggest, to replace many human recruiters with software. The software can apparently predict which applicants will be successful across certain jobs and fast-track them to an interview – without the involvement of a human recruiter.[13] The leaked documents suggest that Amazon believes the new model isn't subject to biases.

Bias in the training data was previously a huge issue for Amazon. But there are other ways in which bias can creep into automated systems. Having a training dataset that's too small is one way. Another is programming the system to rank candidates according to subjective parameters – for example, let's say you determine that having a postgraduate degree is more favourable than just a graduate degree, and you therefore tell the system to prioritize those candidates, that's a subjective decision on your part. By doing what it is told, the system may overlook brilliant candidates who don't have a postgraduate degree. Ranking candidates is a great way to automate recruitment, but you should be careful about the data points you select and ensure you're ranking based on a broad range of criteria.

In another example, an algorithm designed to promote science, technology, engineering, and mathematics (STEM) jobs online prioritized advertising to men purely because women are more expensive to advertise to. Because the system was designed to optimize ad delivery while keeping advertising costs low, it delivered ads to more men than women![14]

Getting automation right

I don't give these examples to put you off recruitment automation. Far from it. I believe the benefits of recruitment automation outweigh the downsides – particularly, and ironically, when it comes to *reducing* the risk of bias and discrimination in recruitment decisions. Human bias is one of the biggest challenges in recruitment. Because, as much as we're supposed to judge people objectively, and most of us set out to do just that, the fact is humans are prone to cognitive bias (however subtle or subconscious it may be). This can be as irrational as disliking a certain phrase or buzzword used by a candidate.

Automation has the potential to take our human bias out of the equation and assess candidates in a truly objective way. But that only works when the data and algorithms are unbiased. Awareness and oversight are your best weapons here – meaning it's really important to be aware of the possible downsides, carefully assess your data for potential bias, and think hard about the assessment criteria used by algorithms. You could, for example, have your algorithms assess candidates purely on a skills basis, and ignore other factors such as age, gender, name and education. You should also implement checks and balances throughout the process, and find a balance between human expertise and machine decision making. Basically, you don't want to be relying solely on what the machine says.

I would also strongly urge you to ensure any automation is as transparent as possible. You don't, for example, want a chatbot to pretend to be a human HR professional. Always be clear with candidates when they're dealing with a machine, how their data is being used, and so on.

Recruitment in the metaverse era

We've touched on the metaverse briefly, but since it's likely to play a larger role in recruitment in future, let's close out the chapter with a quick look at metaverse-based recruitment.

For now, metaverse recruitment is likely to take the shape of virtual recruitment sessions and career fairs, largely aimed at attracting tech-savvy talent, as per the Carrefour event from earlier in the chapter. Other companies to have held metaverse career fairs include Capgemini and Samsung – with the latter enabling job seekers to virtually consult with recruiters (or rather, recruiters' avatars) during the event.[15]

Looking a little further ahead, we may see organizations create their own virtual recruitment centres where candidates attend virtual interviews and assessments. Indeed, the metaverse could simply be the next evolution of gamification in recruitment and selection. Instead of candidates playing, for example, a social media game to assess their suitability for a role, they could immerse themselves in a virtual assessment experience that replicates what they'd face in the real-world role. I could see this being of great interest to, say, hospitality companies and retailers, but it could no doubt prove useful in a vast range of industries.

Adding an extra, more immersive dimension to recruitment and selection is one clear advantage of the metaverse. But another advantage is, quite simply, enhancing your employer brand. For example, if you're trying to attract innovative, creative, tech-savvy people, they're likely to appreciate you taking a similarly innovative, creative, tech-focused approach to your recruitment. It makes sense that recruiting in the metaverse will also prove especially useful for companies who want to hire freelancers and remote employees on a large scale. Because, in the metaverse, you can conduct huge campaigns without geographical borders.

It's still early days for recruiting in the metaverse, but HR professionals should definitely watch this space…

Key takeaways

Let's finish with a quick summary of the main takeaways on intelligent recruitment and selection:

- AI algorithms can identify patterns in large datasets and extract valuable insights that help HR professionals to better match candidates with the requirements of the role, improve the candidate experience and reduce bias in the hiring process.

- The main ways in which data and AI can boost your recruitment activities include improving your employer brand; identifying the best recruitment channels; identifying and assessing the most suitable candidates; and streamlining recruitment with AI-enhanced automation tools.

- Automation in particular can provide massive advantages for HR teams by taking care of the easily repeatable tasks and freeing up recruiters' time for more value-adding activities. Some of the tasks that can be automated include pre-screening candidates, assessing candidates (for example, personality testing), scheduling interviews, sourcing resumes, posting job ads, and more.

- Automation also has the potential to take bias out of the equation and assess candidates in a truly objective way. However, it's important to note that bias can creep into algorithms – for example, if the training dataset is limited. It's therefore extremely important to be aware of the possible downsides, carefully assess your data for potential bias and think hard about assessment criteria.

- Finally, HR professionals should be on the lookout for opportunities to recruit in the metaverse – immersive virtual recruitment fairs, for example, or VR experiences that show what it's really like to work for your company. In the future, more talent will be recruited in this way.

Of course, attracting and hiring the best talent is only part of the challenge; you must also onboard that talent successfully. In the next chapter, we'll explore how data and AI is enhancing the onboarding process.

Notes

1 Randstad RiseSmart. The connection between HR analytics and employer brand, Randstad RiseSmart, nd. info.randstadrisesmart.com/wp-rg-insight-whitepaper (archived at https://perma.cc/W5MF-Z2L4)

2 J Bersin. Data proves that culture, values and career are biggest drivers of employment brand, Josh Bersin, 25 July 2016. joshbersin.com/2016/07/data-proves-that-culture-values-and-career-are-biggest-drivers-of-employment-brand (archived at https://perma.cc/N4KT-B2YH)

3 P-N Schwab. Recruitment in the metaverse: Examples and perspective (analysis), Into The Minds, 25 May 2022. www.intotheminds.com/blog/en/recruitment-metaverse (archived at https://perma.cc/WHG9-594D)

4 B Marr. Walmart: The big data skills crisis and recruiting analytics talent, Forbes, 6 July 2015. www.forbes.com/sites/bernardmarr/2015/07/06/walmart-the-big-data-skills-crisis-and-recruiting-analytics-talent (archived at https://perma.cc/5SNW-8PFV)

5 R Baldwin. Study: Facebook likes can be used to determine intelligence, sexuality, Wired, March 2013. www.wired.com/2013/03/facebook-like-research (archived at https://perma.cc/WFK3-23G9)

6 B Aslan. To all recruiters – use machine learning to hire better candidates, Medium, 18 June 2016. medium.com/@deadlocked_d/to-all-recruiters-use-machine-learning-to-hire-better-candidates-c5aad22f3319 (archived at https://perma.cc/3YJM-YXHF)

7 B Marr. Can big data find your next CEO? Forbes, 27 June 2015. www.forbes.com/sites/bernardmarr/2015/07/27/can-big-data-find-your-next-ceo (archived at https://perma.cc/SQK2-DEBC)

8 M Mahto and D Miller. AI for work relationships may be a great untapped opportunity, Deloitte, 24 October 2022. www2.deloitte.com/uk/en/insights/industry/public-sector/how-social-ai-is-transforming-the-workplace.html (archived at https://perma.cc/R4N6-GQN4)

9 H L Kurter. How Hilton reduced their time to hire from 43 days down to 5, Forbes, 19 September 2019. www.forbes.com/sites/heidilynnekurter/2019/09/19/how-hilton-reduced-their-time-to-hire-from-43-days-down-to-5 (archived at https://perma.cc/R9P4-BZ8Y)

10 Entelo. What is recruiting automation? Entelo, nd. www.entelo.com/recruiting-automation (archived at https://perma.cc/BEQ5-7CWG)

11 Google Cloud. Johnson & Johnson: Reimagining recruiting with Jibe and Google, Google Cloud, nd. cloud.google.com/customers/johnson-and-johnson (archived at https://perma.cc/PPM4-78JK)

12 BBC. Amazon scrapped 'sexist AI' tool, BBC News, 10 October 2018. www.bbc.com/news/technology-45809919 (archived at https://perma.cc/D3JN-32AR)

13 J Del Ray. A leaked Amazon memo may help explain why the tech giant is pushing out so many recruiters, Vox, 23 November 2022. www.vox.com/recode/2022/11/23/23475697/amazon-layoffs-buyouts-recruiters-ai-hiring-software (archived at https://perma.cc/LB22-J4HL)

14 M Lavanchy. Amazon's sexist hiring algorithm could still be better than a human, IMD, November 2018, www.imd.org/research-knowledge/articles/amazons-sexist-hiring-algorithm-could-still-be-better-than-a-human (archived at https://perma.cc/2G95-RBZZ)

15 Multiplier. Hiring in an alternate digital universe with metaverse, Multiplier, nd. www.usemultiplier.com/blog/hiring-in-the-metaverse (archived at https://perma.cc/T8RA-9HJ5)

Improving employee onboarding

08

Onboarding has always been a vital part of the HR function. Indeed, this process of initiating new employees into the company can make or break the employee experience.

Data and AI can play a significant role in onboarding new hires, helping to create a more personalized and engaging experience for new hires – while at the same time saving time and effort through automation. By using data and AI, organizations can enhance the onboarding experience for new hires, increase engagement and retention, and create a more positive impression of the organization. It's no wonder that, according to a 2022 report, 68 per cent of organizations in the US are already using AI in their onboarding processes.[1]

But what does this look like in practice? Let's find out...

Onboarding in the AI era

There are many onboarding software tools out there that promise all sorts of benefits. But, for me, there are two main ways in which these tools can enhance the onboarding process: saving time through automation, and providing a more personalized experience for new hires. It almost seems like a contradiction, doesn't it? That data and AI could on the one hand automate many onboarding processes, and on the other, help to provide a more human experience for employees. But that's exactly the case. Let's explore automation in the first instance, since this is where many efficiencies lie.

Automating aspects of onboarding

While every employee is unique and valued as an individual, there's no denying that onboarding new hires involves a lot of mundane, repetitive tasks that are the same for each and every one. AI can help to reduce the load these processes place on HR professionals, thereby freeing up their time for employee interactions that deliver the most value.

Use cases vary from employer to employer, depending on the size of the organization and the scope of the onboarding programme. But, in general, we're talking about automating simple, easily repeatable tasks. (As we saw in Chapter 7, using software to carry out such tasks is known as *robotic process automation*, and this can be combined with AI for maximum effect.)

Here are some of the tasks that can be automated with onboarding software:

- You can automatically gather required data from new employees.

    o For example, sending requests for pay slips from their previous employment, or proof of identity. (In fact, many of the compliance-related onboarding tasks can be easily automated.) Automated systems can not only handle such communications, but also analyse the resulting data, depending on your needs – for instance, segmenting an employee's data according to demographics. And, for employees, the good news is they only need to provide the required data once, instead of completing multiple forms.

- You can automatically send messages to employees at various stages of their onboarding journey, such as signing the offer letter, sending the employment contract and in the run-up to their first day.

- You can use chatbots to automate certain conversations.

    o Before, during and after a person joins your organization, you'll no doubt have multiple interactions with them that go beyond sending automated welcome messages. In particular, many new hires will have questions they need answering. While not all of these questions can be managed with chatbots, your frequently asked questions can certainly be automated.

- You can use software to automatically create and assign system profiles for new hires – such as creating user accounts and email addresses, and assigning access to internal systems.

- You can automate onboarding checklists.

    o There's typically a long list of items for new hires to do in their first days, weeks and months with the company. AI can automate this checklist process and track the employee's progress against tasks, providing reminders and prompts when tasks remain unchecked.

- You can automate training workflows.

  o Training will obviously be different for different roles within the company, but onboarding software can help to manage the process (for example, by scheduling training or providing reminders). This ensures each employee gains the essential knowledge they need to perform their role – and gets it at the right time.

- Chatbots can be used to informally gather feedback from employees about the onboarding process.

  o Remember that AI can automatically detect the sentiment in written responses, giving you quick insights on how employees feel about the onboarding process, and helping to pinpoint where people may need extra support.

- You can also automatically analyse the progress and performance of new hires. (We'll talk more about performance management in Chapter 9.)

- You can even use AI to help new hires boost their network and get to know helpful colleagues.

  o AI tools can make suggestions for each employee on which personnel or team leaders they might want to get to know, based on their role and training needs.

- All of these tasks apply to onboarding remote hires, as well.

  o AI tools can also help you provide tailored support to remote employees. For example, AI can be used to automatically translate onboarding documents and communications into another language. (What's more, thanks to the metaverse, you can deliver a highly immersive virtual onboarding experience. More on the metaverse coming up later.)

- And don't forget that you can also automate reporting on your onboarding trends and patterns, thanks to HR analytics tools (Chapter 6).

It's worth noting that many of the above examples can also be applied when employees are promoted or transitioning to a new role within the company, when people rejoin the organization after a career break and even when people leave the business altogether.

If you are able to automate onboarding processes, you stand to reap several benefits. The most obvious is decreasing the HR workload and time spent on mundane tasks – which, in turn, allows HR professionals to focus their time on more strategic tasks. Automation also speeds up the onboarding process, thereby allowing new hires to reach productivity more quickly. And, most importantly, the onboarding experience is consistent and positive for all new employees. With templates and automated workflows, nothing gets overlooked and everyone enjoys the same initial experience. So, while it's true that setting up automated systems requires an investment of time and money, the long-term pay-off can be significant.

Creating a more engaging, personal onboarding experience

Because so much of onboarding involves routine, task-based processes, it can very easily feel impersonal to the employee joining the organization. An exercise in ticking boxes on a list and little more. While it may seem counterintuitive, AI can be used to inject a little more personalization into the onboarding journey, making it feel more human and welcoming.

In fact, one of the things I like most about data is it allows for so much personalization. When you're automatically tracking and monitoring the employee onboarding process, you gather a wealth of information on how that employee is doing and how they feel about the onboarding process. Used well, this information can help you create a more personalized, engaging onboarding process that's tailored to each individual – and, in turn, promotes a positive impression of the organization.

As an example, AI can leverage data from onboarding surveys and automated chats (not to mention social media and other data sources) to gain insights into new hires' preferences, strengths, and areas they wish to develop. This information can be used to tailor onboarding programmes to meet the unique needs of each individual, providing them with relevant and meaningful content that plugs gaps in their learning – or better aligns with their goals and interests.

To put it another way, AI tools can be used to connect new hires with the right people, right information and right resources, all at the right time.

But to achieve this you'll need data, and plenty of it. You'll need to be collecting data throughout the hiring process, throughout the onboarding process and from your existing workforce. And you'll need to be taking the temperature of employees on a regular basis, so that you can gauge sentiment and track progress. Not only should you use all this data to deliver a more personalized onboarding experience for new hires, you should also use it to refine your onboarding experience in general. If the same feedback is coming from multiple employees, for example, that gives you an opportunity to refine the experience for everyone in future.

What about the downsides of AI in onboarding?

As with any use of AI, you need to be aware of the potential pitfalls. The good news about onboarding – compared to, say, recruitment – is it's largely objective (by which I mean the same tasks are carried out at the same time for all new hires). So there's less opportunity in general for bias to creep into automated onboarding processes. Good news.

Perhaps the biggest challenge, then, is finding the right balance between the human element and the tasks that are best delegated to machines. Data and AI should not replace the role of human HR professionals in initiating new people into the business – rather, it should be used as a way to allow HR professionals to focus their time where it has the most impact. Sending requests for documentation or confirmation letters to multiple new hires is something that can easily be handed over to machines. But it's vital that employees receive a genuinely human welcome to the organization. From interviews and reviews to mentorship opportunities, there are plenty of touchpoints where the human element is absolutely vital.

Bottom line, you should seek to automate those mundane, easily repeatable tasks, while recognizing that humans will always be needed in the onboarding process.

Onboarding new hires in the metaverse

If we can recruit people in the metaverse (see Chapter 7), why not onboard them in the metaverse as well? While this won't apply to all employees or all tasks in the onboarding journey, it's certainly worth considering the metaverse as an onboarding tool – especially for remote hires who will never set foot in your office.

What do we mean by onboarding in the metaverse? Well, as the metaverse is evolving so rapidly, there are no hard and fast rules. But, in general, we're talking about providing immersive, virtual onboarding experiences that mimic 'being there' in person. Think virtual meetings or virtual training sessions that provide a more engaging experience than your average Zoom call. Onboarding in this way – especially for remote hires – can make the process feel more fun and help to foster a deeper connection with the organization.

You can even take remote onboarding to a whole new level and create a *digital twin* of your real-world office – a virtual space that looks exactly like the office that new hires encounter in the real world. This could be used to provide virtual tours (useful for any new hire who will be joining the office in person, so they can orient themselves before their first day), or a realistic-looking space where new hires can meet team members or colleagues.

It's early days for metaverse onboarding, but one company leading the way is Accenture. The IT services and consulting giant has created a virtual campus known as One Accenture Park, located in what Accenture calls 'the Nth Floor' (basically, the company's metaverse presence). Resembling a corporate theme park, One Accenture Park features a virtual boardroom and conference room, with a virtual zip line that whizzes the employee (or rather, the employee's personalized digital avatar) off to different destinations in the virtual campus.

In the past, the onboarding process at Accenture involved new employees meeting senior leaders and other colleagues in face-to-face meetings. But that wasn't possible during the pandemic. So One Accenture Park was designed to offer a more immersive place for new hires to learn and network with colleagues – all they have to do is don their VR headset.

Accenture says this isn't designed to replace real-world interactions between employees.[2] Rather, the metaverse campus provides a focused space for new hires to meet with leaders and colleagues – without the distraction of emails and notifications, as is often the case in the physical world.

It's not just about networking, though. In One Accenture Park, new employees can learn in a more fun, interactive way, thanks to a wealth of onboarding materials and exercises. For example, they can ascend the 'leadership mountain' attraction in the park while learning the fundaments of effective management. There's a 'phishing pier' where employees can learn cybersecurity awareness. There are also realistic virtual replicas of Accenture's physical offices so new employees can learn their way around. (These can also be used by any employees for virtual meetings.)

Unconvinced of the metaverse's potential to deliver information to new hires? Consider the 2019 study from a group at the University of Nottingham, UK, which researched the effectiveness of VR training versus a traditional PowerPoint training session. The researchers found that those who participated in VR training had better levels of engagement and long-term retention of information than those who endured the dreaded PowerPoint.[3] Accenture has noticed similar results; the company says that providing interactive training in the metaverse improved the retention of information by 33 per cent.[4] Importantly, employees seem to love it – with Accenture's virtual onboarding experience receiving a feedback rating of 4.7 out of 5. With feedback like that, it would be daft to ignore the potential of the metaverse to provide a better onboarding experience.

Key takeaways

To summarize the main points from this chapter:

- Data and AI can play a significant role in onboarding new hires, helping to create a more personalized and engaging experience for new hires – while at the same time saving time and effort through automation.

- When it comes to automation, some of the tasks that can be carried out by software bots include sending standard communications, answering frequently asked questions (FAQs), collecting feedback during the onboarding process, and more. This frees up HR professionals' time, allowing them to focus on employee interactions that have the most impact.

- AI can also be used to inject more personalization into the onboarding journey, making it feel more human and welcoming. AI can leverage data from onboarding surveys and automated chats, for example, to gain insights into new hires' preferences, strengths and areas for improvement. This can be used to tailor onboarding programmes to meet the unique needs of each individual.

- It's really important to find the right balance between those tasks that should be allocated to machines, and those that require the human touch. So, while you should absolutely seek to automate mundane, easily repeatable tasks, remember that human HR professionals will always be needed in the onboarding process.

- Finally, for many employers, the metaverse could provide exciting new ways to deliver orientation and training sessions – providing an immersive onboarding experience, while improving knowledge retention.

It's clear that data and AI can help to smooth the onboarding journey. But once an employee is established in their role, how can data and AI be used to boost their performance? Turn to Chapter 9 to find out.

Notes

1 Leena AI. The state of employee onboarding in the US, Leena AI, 2022. leena.ai/ state-of-employee-onboarding-united-states (archived at https://perma.cc/BK6C-WL7Z)

2 O Pickup. Why more companies are sending new hires straight to the metaverse for improve onboarding, Work Life, 17 June 2022. www.worklife.news/technology/why-more-companies-are-sending-new-hires-straight-to-the-metaverse-for-improved-onboarding (archived at https://perma.cc/QMH3-QDFB)

3 University of Nottingham. Study finds virtual reality training could improve employee safety, EurekAlert, 16 September 2019. www.eurekalert.org/news-releases/530825 (archived at https://perma.cc/9N65-Q428)

4 HRM. How Accenture is onboarding its employees in the metaverse, HRM, 7 December 2022. www.hrmonline.com.au/onboarding/accenture-onboards-employees-in-the-metaverse (archived at https://perma.cc/7B67-4FKL)

Performance monitoring and management 09

Generally speaking, measuring and reviewing the performance of employees is done poorly by many companies. Traditional methods such as annual performance reviews are often disliked by both the employees being reviewed and the managers conducting the reviews, and can be a huge waste of time.

Thankfully, new approaches driven by data and AI are allowing HR teams to optimize employee performance monitoring and management, and gain valuable insights into employee productivity, performance, engagement and areas for improvement. By leveraging data from various sources – such as HR systems, performance reviews and employee feedback – AI algorithms can identify performance trends, patterns and correlations, allowing HR professionals to gain a deeper understanding of what drives employee performance. This information can then be used to develop more targeted and effective performance management strategies, such as personalized coaching, goal-setting and recognition programmes. AI-powered performance management systems can also provide real-time feedback and performance metrics, allowing employees to monitor their progress and receive actionable insights for improvement. Furthermore, data and AI can be used to identify high-performing employees and potential successors, allowing organizations to develop talent pipelines and succession plans.

As we'll see in this chapter, organizations can now use data and AI to create a more objective, transparent and effective performance management process, improve employee engagement and retention, and drive better business outcomes.

A quick word of warning before we start

Measuring people performance with data and analytics can bring many benefits, but it must be applied carefully. Because there's a fine line between performance improvement and employee surveillance, and companies that have overstepped this mark have faced huge backlashes. Most people don't want their boss to monitor their every move, and in fact this can be hugely demoralizing for staff, particularly the most self-motivated members of the workforce. To avoid your company coming across as some sort of Orwellian tyrant, you'll need to tread a fine line, gathering the data that you really need to give people genuinely useful feedback, without freaking out your workforce or damaging your employer brand.

Therefore, it is vitally important you ensure that data and AI are used ethically, transparently and with human oversight to a) avoid unintended consequences and b) maintain a human-centric approach to performance management. This is a difficult balance to achieve and maintain, no doubt about it, and my concern is that many employers won't get this delicate balance right. We'll talk more about this topic later in the chapter and explore how you can find the appropriate balance for your organization. But I wanted to flag this topic now so you can keep it at the front of your mind as you read the chapter.

Lessons from the world of sports

Why start with sports, you ask? Well, sport is often at the cutting edge of data and analytics, and it provides a useful glimpse of how data can be used to drive very real performance improvements. Coaches across a whole range of sports, from cycling to football, are using data to assess and improve individual performance.

Measuring physical performance and sleep

A number of NFL American football teams use an athlete tracking system called OptimEye, developed by Catapult Sports. A lightweight wearable device (worn in a small top that looks a bit like a sports bra) tracks metrics such as players' speed, motion and heart rate, and calculates player exertion. Having this data helps coaches and support staff identify which players are working hardest in practice and who could work harder, as well as prevent illness or injuries from players pushing themselves too hard. It also means workouts and practice drills can be tailored to each individual on the team. Plus, if a player does get injured, the historical data will help ensure the player doesn't reinjure themselves during recovery.

Such devices are also used in the UK by many soccer teams to monitor and design individual training routines, and spot early warning signs of injury. Looking to the future, devices are being developed to monitor factors like adrenaline and cortisol (the stress hormone) levels, as well as perspiration levels.

But sport performance isn't just about physical exertion; good quality sleep is another critical factor in getting athletes to perform at their best. A Stanford University study found that basketball players who slept for an extra 90 minutes improved both the accuracy of their shots and how fast they could run.[1] In football, many clubs give players wristbands to assess sleep quality, in order to assess any potential problems and find solutions that will help boost the player's performance.

Moving to real-time analysis

When it comes to analysing player performance in matches, most analysis was traditionally done post-match using video analytics. Not anymore. In 2015, the International Football (soccer) Association Board agreed to change the rules governing the use of wearable devices, opening up the potential for league and competition organizers to allow players to wear such devices during matches themselves. This provides coaching teams with a wealth of new possibilities to track actual player performance during a match and potentially make changes at half-time based on what the data is telling them. The hope is that the use of tracking devices would also help reduce the number of deaths from cardiac arrest.

While in-depth monitoring like this clearly goes way beyond what the average company is capable of, the use of cheap and readily available fitness trackers could change this. It's not inconceivable, for example, for employers to use sleep data to understand who may be too tired for a certain job, especially if it's a dangerous task. Even in a typical office setting, a critical sales pitch or meeting could be allocated to the employee who is the most rested.

Intelligently measuring employee performance

There's clear evidence that measuring performance delivers very real operational and financial improvements, as the UPS example later in this chapter shows. However, 'performance' is the critical word in that sentence – companies need to make it clear they're monitoring *performance* and not individual *behaviour*.

This is important because, thanks to the sheer amount of data we can now gather on employees, it's possible for HR teams to understand more about their employees than ever before – including how they think, what they're feeling, who they interact with and how productive they are. To improve people performance in a meaningful way without alienating your workforce, it's important to drill down to the right metrics that will drive performance while maintaining employee engagement. This is likely to involve looking at metrics such as which factors motivate employees, what stops them performing at their best, where people are dissatisfied in the organization and so on, rather than metrics like how many hours employees spend at their desk or how long they spend in the bathroom.

In this way, data-driven, intelligent performance management is about finding a more grown-up way of measuring performance, where intelligent people understand exactly what they need to do to help the company succeed, and data is used to see how this is going in reality.

The Internet of Things – and how happy, connected employees are more productive

The rise of Internet of Things-enabled devices, particularly wearables, plays a huge role in HR's ability to effectively measure performance. This can mean measuring physical movements, such as how staff are coping in challenging physical conditions (there's more on employee safety and wellbeing in Chapter 11), or how people are interacting with each other, such as the IoT-enabled smart employee badges that we saw in Chapter 3.

Using technology to drive efficiency isn't a new thing. In the 1990s, telecoms company Bell Canada gave phone technicians devices to wear on their wrists that let them enter repair data without having to go back to the computer in their vehicle. And this reportedly saved each technician almost an hour a day.[2] But this technology has leapt forward with modern wearables, such as employee badges and wrist bands.

What particularly interests me is how wearables can help measure and improve both productivity and wellbeing. After all, happy employees are more productive, and connectivity plays an important role in this. In one example, Bank of America used wearable technology to measure employee activities, and found that call centre workers who took breaks together were happier than those who didn't. So the company instituted a group break policy, and saw a double-digit bump in productivity as a result.[3] This a great example of using data and analytics to drive employee performance in a positive, thoughtful way.

Wearables are also helping employees work smarter. (Note I said 'smarter' not 'faster.') One example comes from digital consulting company Accenture, which helped Airbus boost productivity in one specific part of the business by a whopping 500 per cent.[4] They deployed wearable devices call 'head-up displays' to help component assembly workers access assembly information quickly, whenever they needed it. As a result, workers were able to assemble more components more quickly and with dramatically fewer errors.

Other data-driven performance measurement systems

Aside from wearable devices, there are a number of different technologies to help you measure performance. Once again, I want to stress that the idea behind this should be to help individuals and the company as a whole perform better, not to punish individuals who aren't performing well. If someone isn't performing a task as well as expected, there may be a very good reason, from fatigue or stress to systems not working properly or impeding what the employee is trying to do. Data and analysis should help get at the *why* of performance metrics, as well as the *what*.

Tracking computer usage has become relatively commonplace. Indeed, it's now possible to measure virtually everything an employee does on their computer. Software from Veriato, for example, logs web browsing, document use, email use, chat applications and keystrokes, and takes regular screen grabs that are stored for a certain period of time. It also has the potential to alert managers when certain thresholds are met. Personally, I think this is edging very close to the line between what's acceptable for boosting performance and what's infringing on individual privacy – more on that coming up later. However, speaking to *The Wall Street Journal*, one Veriato client said the system delivered real benefits. Celeste O'Keefe, CEO of Dancel Multimedia, uses the system to measure a team of 16, made up of animators, artists, administrators and salespeople. O'Keefe felt the system allows her team to be more streamlined and focused, and she finds it useful for guiding her people in the right direction. O'Keefe uses the system to skim graphs and screengrabs to spot problems with employee productivity. Often these are the result of someone not being familiar with certain software or systems – thus identifying opportunities for training and guidance. However, O'Keefe also acknowledges that her using the system has led to at least one firing.[5]

The market is also awash with productivity tools and apps that monitor performance without necessarily tracking the employee's every move. One example comes from Basecamp, productivity and project management software that allows staff to add their upcoming tasks for the day, week or month and tick them off as and when they're completed. This allows managers to easily see what people are working on and how much they're able to get done. Similarly, the Asana app allows managers to assign tasks and track their progress in real time. For sales teams, Salesforce details how many sales calls and emails were made in a day and how much revenue has been generated from that activity. Tools like these can drastically help to cut down the amount of time managers and staff need to spend emailing each other with updates on projects or holding team meetings.

Going a step further, there are also AI tools that can help you *predict* performance. AI capabilities mean it's now possible to identify characteristics and activities that are linked to high and low performance, and predict relationships between factors like employee characteristics, training investment, employee engagement and performance. For example, predictive analytics firm iNostix (now a Deloitte company) provides predictive systems that it claims can lead to faster time-to-contribution, predict organizational effectiveness, accurately assess employee engagement and predict absenteeism or the risk of workplace accidents.

Intelligently reviewing employee performance (and not on an annual basis)

The way that many companies manage employee performance is through traditional annual reviews that evaluate employees against certain key performance indicators (KPIs). Yet, in today's fast-paced, technology-driven workplaces, annual performance appraisals just aren't working any more. Business moves so much faster these days. It's no surprise that one study indicated that only 6 per cent of companies thought their performance management processes were working.[6] To me, the traditional performance review model is a perfect example of how *not* to review performance because, by its very nature, the process involves looking backwards far more than looking forwards. Plus, employees dislike annual reviews because they usually have to fill out lengthy questionnaires, and managers dislike them because they're incredibly time consuming. In fact, an organization's productivity can dip as much as 40 per cent during the annual review period.[7]

Now, companies are starting to move away from annual reviews, generating more regular discussions and looking to the future rather than the past. Data-driven performance reviewing should be about creating an ongoing dialogue between employees and management, all based on and facilitated by data and evidence. This may include using AI-driven systems and conducting much more regular (but shorter) reviews, as we'll see throughout this section.

A word on linking incentives to performance

Before we get into that, although designing incentive schemes is beyond the scope of this book, I think it's important to note that data-driven employee performance isn't about simply hardwiring KPIs and performance reviews to the incentive system. So many companies design narrow metrics that drive all the wrong employee behaviours; when people know they're being evaluated on certain metrics only, those are the activities they focus on, sometimes to the detriment of other value-building activities. Say, for example, I ask my children to tidy their room and promise a cinema trip in return, but they know I only evaluate how tidy the floor is and never look under the bed or in the cupboard. Which areas do you think they'll tidy and which will they ignore? It's obvious, isn't it? And yet employee reviews and incentives are often designed the same way. That's why, in my mind, it's better to focus on *outcomes* rather than narrow metrics – meaning, if the company is performing well and individuals are contributing to that success, then they should be rewarded accordingly.

CASE STUDY How big employers are overhauling performance reviews

A number of big companies, such as Accenture and Deloitte, have done away with the dreaded annual performance review and revamped their review processes. It's no wonder. In a survey Deloitte itself conducted, it found that more than half of executives did not believe their employee review systems drove employee performance or engagement.[8]

But what do these companies use in place of annual reviews, rankings systems and 360-feedback models? The new systems generally focus on the employee in his or her own role, as opposed to ranking employees against one another or comparing performance to other employees. The focus is therefore on generating a richer, nuanced view of every employee to facilitate better performance.

Such systems also provide feedback much more often. Rather than a single review once a year, they tend to conduct more frequent reviews, at the end of each major project or every month, for example. More frequent check-ins and reviews mean that a manager has more opportunities to steer an employee towards his or her best performance. These more regular reviews typically take far less time to complete. Deloitte, for example, distilled its performance reviews down to just four questions, two of which require yes or no answers.[9] This new breed of performance evaluations also focus on looking to the future, instead of past performance. Rather than reviewing an entire year's performance at one go, these shorter, more frequent reviews are designed to help employees move forward with their careers rather than look back on past accomplishments or failures. This means people are no longer dwelling on what happened in the past, but instead focusing on how to improve in the future.

One major problem with standard performance reviews is that a reviewer's assessment of an employee's skills often says more about the reviewer than the employee. But these new ways of reviewing performance help to remove subjectivity from the process. For example, to combat potential bias, Deloitte changed their questions to ask what a manager would *do* with a person (promote them, incentivize them, etc.) rather than what they *think* of that person.

The use of AI in performance reviews

It's fair to say that many companies have moved away from traditional, metric-based performance assessment in recent years. Sometimes this is because such systems have been found limiting. But sometimes it's because employers and managers are too easily inclined to simply ignore them, if the findings don't line up with their personal 'gut feeling' on who they like or dislike.

Much of the difficulty in assessing performance lies in navigating workplace biases. These are well-documented conscious or unconscious behaviours that can unfairly influence an assessment of an individual's contribution to an organization. Race and gender are perhaps two of the most obvious sources of individual bias (and fortunately often quite easy to spot). Others, however, are more ephemeral, and it may not be so immediately obvious when they are occurring.

One is known as contrast bias, meaning an assessor is inclined to compare an individual's performance to his or her peers, rather than to defined standards of achievement. Another is recency bias, where actions in the recent past are given more weight, perhaps unfairly, than actions which happened further back in time (but still within the period where performance is being assessed). AI-driven tools can help remove bias from the equation and build an objective picture of employee performance.

Another great thing about AI is that it won't treat the job of performance reviews as something to do 'when I've got time'. Unlike many human managers, it won't put off assessments until the last minute – tell it you want an ongoing, 360-degree view of your workforce's effectiveness and (in theory) that's what you'll get.

And because AI-driven assessment can happen in real time (with systems monitoring targets, quotas and how these are affected by people's connections), incentives and praise for good performance can be dished out immediately. If targets are not being met or performance standards are slipping, then intervention can take place before the problem grows and becomes unmanageable.

Using generative AI to write employee performance reviews?

At the time of writing, I'm seeing a trend emerge for using AI tools – in particular, the AI chatbot, ChatGPT – to write employee performance reviews. The thinking behind this is to save managers' time (because they need only give the system brief feedback prompts, and it then writes that up into a more comprehensive review).

While I'm in favour of using AI to analyse and boost performance, I'm wary of using generative AI tools to actually write performance reviews. Feedback should come from a manager, not a machine.

Besides, it's relatively early days for tools like ChatGPT and they may not always work in the way we intend. As an example, in one experiment using

ChatGPT to write performance reviews, the resulting reviews were found to be 'wildly sexist'.[10] The chatbot had a tendency to impart gendered feedback into otherwise neutral information. Kindergarten teachers and nurses, for example, were presumed to be female while construction workers and engineers were presumed to be male. This happened in some – not all – cases when the system wasn't given any information on the gender of the employee. When the system *was* told the gender of employees, it consistently wrote longer, more critical feedback for women compared to male colleagues in the same job with the same feedback input.

And even when the system did deliver gender-neutral feedback, it was so generic it wouldn't be that helpful for employees anyway (for instance, it was lacking in examples from the employee's work). But, as I said, it's early days for using AI to generate performance reviews, and it will be very interesting to see how the technology develops.

Implementing more regular, or even continual, feedback loops

We know that short 'pulse' surveys can be used to gather more regular feedback from employees on how they feel about the company. But this process works both ways. As well as the company benefitting from regular employee feedback, employees themselves benefit from regular feedback. Such feedback, be it from a line manager, peers or a mentor, helps employees understand their performance, feel recognized for their contribution and feel more connected with the company, thereby boosting engagement.

As an example, BetterWorks's AI-driven tool is designed to increase the frequency of feedback. Its AI algorithms can be used to track employee goals and progress, and provide comments, nudges and recognition where needed. The system then prompts feedback from the relevant people, such as a line manager. Importantly, the system also recognizes an individual's preferences for feedback and interactions, such as real-time feedback notifications or batches of notifications. Solutions like this, which provide instant or very regular feedback, could provide the ideal solution to the problem of annual reviews based on data that's already out of date. Managers can evaluate performance and deliver feedback based on real-time data, and employees can get helpful feedback and recognition also in real time.

Peer feedback is another growing aspect of performance reviews. Tools are now available that deliver continuous (or regular), anonymous peer feedback to employees, sometimes with recommendations to help them improve their performance. Tools like this allow team members to communicate openly and regularly with each other, and help employees identify their strengths and opportunities for growth and improvement. And for managers and HR teams, these systems can help them understand wider skills, strengths and areas for improvement.

However, employee peer review systems need to be approached with caution. When used as part of an employee ranking system, which pits employees against each other, they can be open to abuse and attempts to rig the rankings by delivering negative feedback on peers. But, used carefully, it's easy to see how open, supportive feedback from peers could help individuals improve their performance, grow as employees and achieve their potential.

Lessons from Amazon: How *not* to handle people monitoring and reviews

These instances stem from a few years back, but they remain memorable (and not in a good way) examples of how *not* to monitor and manage employee performance.

Tracking every move

In the UK, working conditions at Amazon's distribution centres have made national news in the past, with stories of workers reportedly walking up to 15 miles during a shift, having their every move monitored by GPS tracking tags, and having just 30 minutes to walk the equivalent of nine football pitches to get to the canteen, eat lunch and get back to the warehouse.[11] The company reportedly had the ability to monitor staff every minute they were on site, including their precise location in the warehouse, exactly how many items they picked or packed, and even how many bathroom breaks they took and for how long. This delivered huge efficiencies for Amazon, but potentially might have harmed their employer brand in the UK.

Huge workloads and secret feedback

In addition, the retailer's feedback culture came in for significant criticism in a 2015 *New York Times* article, which focused on the company's headquarters in Seattle.[12] The article, which featured interviews with many ex-Amazon employees, described a 'bruising' feedback culture that encourages employees to criticize colleagues' ideas and send secret feedback to their managers.

According to the article, every new employee had to subscribe to fourteen leadership principles, from the not-so-unusual like 'think big' to the slightly ominous sounding 'disagree and commit' and 'frugality'. While many employees spoke positively of how that helped them excel, other interviewees described a culture where huge workloads and pressure are commonplace, with one saying she didn't sleep for four straight days and others reporting working at nights, on weekends and on holidays.

According to the article, the harsh performance review culture included weekly or monthly reviews where individual employees were given lengthy reports (sometimes 50 or 60 pages) on the various metrics that they were being held accountable for. They were then quizzed on various aspects of the report.

But it's the internal feedback tool that perhaps raises the most eyebrows. Called the Anytime Feedback Tool, this system allows employees to send positive or negative feedback about their colleagues to management. It's a system open to abuse. Team members are ranked, and those scoring lowest were (at the time of the article) reportedly eliminated each year, which meant employees effectively competed against each other for their jobs and everyone felt they had to outperform everyone else.

Average employee tenure is just one year

It's perhaps no wonder that a PayScale survey ranked Amazon second on a list of companies with high staff turnover.[13] According to the data, Amazon employees stick around on average for just one year – one of the very briefest tenures in the Fortune 500. At the time of the article, Amazon founder and then CEO Jeff Bezos responded by writing a memo to Amazon staff stating that the article didn't reflect the culture he knew, and asked staff to report any unfair practices to HR.[14] But the high staff turnover indicates that the internal feedback system has had a negative effect on employee satisfaction.

For me, one of the main problems with the Amazon feedback system was not just that employees felt driven to outperform each other, but that their access to peer feedback filtered down only from their managers (employees could not see the feedback sent about them whenever they wanted – it had to be delivered via a manager). To really help employees grow and improve, they should be able to ask for or access feedback when they need it, like the continuous performance review systems seen earlier in this chapter.

CASE STUDY   Lessons from UPS: How to drive performance
without alienating people

With vehicle sensors and GPS data, it's possible to know exactly where delivery drivers are, which route they're taking or how fast they're driving, and many companies are routinely using this sort of data to improve driver behaviour and optimize delivery routes. UPS, however, has taken the use of data and analytics to a whole new level. For example, the handheld computer that drivers have been carrying for years (those electronic boxes you sign to say you received your parcel) is actually a sophisticated device that helps drivers make better decisions, such as which order to deliver parcels in for the most efficient route.

But it's the delivery trucks themselves that provide a wealth of data about driver performance. UPS trucks are fitted with more than 200 sensors that gather data on everything from whether the driver is wearing a seatbelt, or when the back doors are open, to how long the vehicle spends idling as opposed to in motion, and how many times the driver has to reverse or make a U-turn.

Big benefits from data

With so many drivers on the road, improving driver performance so they drive as efficiently as possible means big savings for UPS. The company has said that shaving just one minute off the time each driver spends idling as opposed to in motion saves over $500,000 in fuel across the whole fleet. UPS has also said that same minute adds up to operational savings of $14.6 million a year.[15] One insight gained from the sensor data was that drivers opening the truck door with a key was slowing them down and eating up valuable time. So the company gave drivers a key fob with a simple push-button to open the doors much quicker. Tiny time savings like this make a huge difference across a fleet the size of UPS.

And the savings are clear. By monitoring their drivers and providing feedback and training where needed, UPS has achieved a reduction of 8.5 million gallons of fuel and 85 million miles per year.[16] Plus, while drivers now make an average of 120 stops a day, that number used to be less than 100 – meaning the same drivers with the same trucks are now able to deliver significantly more packages than they used to.

Protecting and rewarding employees

This increased performance has been reflected by increased wages, with UPS drivers now earning around twice what they did in the mid-1990s.[17] The company is widely regarded as the biggest and most efficient parcel shipper in the world – largely thanks to its innovative use of data – and its drivers are among the best paid in the industry. That no doubt helps support employee buy-in for monitoring so much of what drivers do. But the company has also had to take other steps to ensure they don't face a huge backlash from drivers; for example, under the terms of drivers' contracts, UPS cannot collect data without informing drivers of what they're gathering. And nor can they discipline a driver based only on what the data has told them. Sensible safeguards like this would work for almost any type of performance data in any industry. When implemented and properly followed, such safeguards help facilitate employee buy-in, ensure transparency and minimize the risk of damage to morale or employer brand.

Finding the right balance between trusting and tracking

It should be clear by now that I'm talking about using data and AI to enable performance, not surveil your employees. Since I wrote the first edition of this book, I've noticed a clear rise in the use of productivity monitoring tools that track employees' computer use in incredible detail, right down to keyboard and mouse activity. This has grown enormously since the pandemic, as companies allow more people to work remotely. (The implication being 'If we can't see you, how can we trust you to do the work?')

The slippery slope to surveillance

According to *The New York Times*, many remote workers have even reported being paid only for the minutes where they were actively working at their computer (backed up by screenshots of the computer and photographs of the employee sat there).[18] So, minutes where they made a cup of coffee, went to the bathroom, sat back and read an offline document related to their job, or answered the door to sign for a package, were deducted from their payable hours.

Incidentally, the same *New York Times* investigation found that eight of the ten largest US employers were doing some form of 'individual employee productivity monitoring', often in real time. And we're not just talking about the monitoring of employees who are low down on the corporate food chain – many are highly experienced, highly paid employees. At New York's Metropolitan Transit Authority, for instance, employees such as engineers and lawyers were told they could work from home one day a week, providing they agreed to full-time productivity monitoring – so, not just on the days they were at home but all the time. While some workers spoken to by *The New York Times* praised monitoring software for making things 'fair' and ensuring their contribution was seen, the majority weren't impressed. I don't blame them.

This level of employee monitoring is essentially *surveillance*. As someone who works from home almost all of the time, I find this sort of approach at best infantilizing, and at worst it is an infringement of personal privacy. Consider, for a moment, what motivates you as an employee and what would send your satisfaction and engagement plummeting. Would having your photo taken at your desk every 10 minutes and bathroom breaks monitored motivate you to perform at your best?

Personally, I'm very self-motivated – give me a goal and I'll achieve it. If I felt my boss was tracking my every move to make sure I achieved that goal, I would hardly thrive. If we think of the publisher of this book as my boss for a second, I know I wouldn't be happy if my 'boss' was monitoring how many minutes I spent typing at my computer. On paper, those minutes spent 'idling' and not typing would look unproductive, and yet those minutes are critically important for research and organizing my thoughts. If my every keystroke was monitored, I'd feel extremely demotivated and disengaged. Not only that, while such monitoring may lead me (at least in the short term) to produce more words per day, the quality of my output would likely go down, not up. That's the danger with monitoring employees – self-motivated employees could well be put off and you could end up with the opposite effect to what you intended.

In other words, it's really important to find the right balance between trusting your employees and monitoring their performance. And this goes for remote workers *and* those who are based on site. You want to *enable* great performance, rather than *control* employees' activities. If we refer back to the world of sports for a moment, data is used to enable players and athletes to perform at their best – it's not used to micromanage and control individual behaviour or as a tool to punish poor performance.

Sure, sometimes you do need to monitor and manage an employee a little more closely than usual – especially when there's been a problem with performance – but, for the most part, your goal is to enable people to make better decisions and achieve their potential.

Avoiding employee backlash

As well as the risk of demoralizing employees, there are legitimate privacy concerns about monitoring employee performance. Employees have a right to privacy, after all, and that must be carefully managed alongside the need to better understand their performance. Improper use of data (see Chapter 4) can not only tarnish your employer brand, but it could potentially land you in legal trouble.

Say, for example, that employees wear badges that track their interactions with customers and other staff. A manager could potentially use this information to identify which member of their team went to HR with a complaint. If the manager then fired that employee, with no other grounds, the employee would have an excellent case for unfair dismissal. Or, if employees are wearing fitness tracking devices, for example, there is a danger that health data could be used to discriminate against those who are less physically healthy, regardless of how well they perform in the job.

One real-life example of employee monitoring backfiring came from British newspaper the *Daily Telegraph* back in 2016. Journalists reportedly arrived at work one morning to find motion sensors had been installed under their desks, without any warning or explanation whatsoever.[19] The employees' union got involved and the newspaper's management quickly removed the devices. I find it pretty shocking that this measure wasn't communicated to staff prior to the installation – if it had been handled better, they could have avoided all the uproar.

As well as communicating performance-monitoring measures to employees, it's also really important to remember that *improved performance* and *increased output* aren't necessarily the same thing. If all you're doing is trying to increase output, with no consideration of employee wellbeing and engagement, it's likely to backfire and lead to increased stress. And that's especially true in today's fast-paced working environment, where 77 per cent of people say they have experienced burnout on at least one occasion.[20]

Surveillance can have other negative consequences

Alienating your employees and increasing the risk of burnout are two potential downsides of surveilling employees. But that's not all. One study found that employee surveillance can, surprisingly, lead employees to break the rules, not follow them. The researchers found that US employees who were under surveillance took more unapproved breaks, intentionally worked more slowly and even stole more office equipment than colleagues who weren't under surveillance.[21] To test their theory and prove causation, rather than correlation, the researchers carried out a second study in which workers were given a set of tasks to complete as well as the opportunity to cheat. And it turned out, people who knew they were under surveillance were more likely to cheat on their tasks. Why? Those who took part in the study reported feeling a lack of agency and personal responsibility. Monitoring employees too closely can remove people's sense of agency and even create the very behaviours you don't want to see in the workplace.

So, how can you strike the right balance?

Here are six simple best practice guidelines to help you walk the fine line between legitimately useful performance measurement and downright surveillance:

1 **Be transparent.** Be transparent with your employees about exactly what data you collect and how you intend to use it. Be specific on how this will benefit them and help improve company performance overall. Make it clear it's about looking at performance, not watching over every little thing employees do, and that it would never be used to punish individuals.

2 **Minimize the data you collect.** Practise thoughtful data minimization and only collect the data you need to have a genuine impact on performance. You should always be able to justify exactly why you need certain data. If there's no good business case for collecting it, don't do it.

3 **Get consent.** You must ask your employees for consent to use their performance data. And, once you've got consent, only use data for the purpose for which employees have given consent.

4 **Work with the union.** If your employees are members of a union, like UPS drivers, you'll need to consult with the union and gain agreement on performance measurement practices before you implement any measures.

5 **Maintain dialogue.** Keep your employees informed when you make any changes as to what data is gathered and how it's used. Just because you got their buy-in once, doesn't give you carte blanche to monitor anything you like in future.

6 **Demonstrate clear benefits from the data.** Be vocal about successes and show how data-driven performance measuring and reviewing improves the bottom line and helps the company meet its goals – just as in the UPS example. And when improved employee performance delivers better financial performance for the company as a whole, reward your people accordingly.

Key takeaways

Clearly, this is one of the trickier areas of data-driven HR, and a lot of careful thought is needed on what's right for your organization and what will enable your employees to perform at their best. Here's what we've learned in this chapter:

- There's a wafer-thin line between performance improvement and employee surveillance, and companies that have overstepped this mark have faced huge backlashes. Done badly, measuring performance can destroy employee motivation.

- You should be looking to uncover which factors motivate employees, what stops them performing at their best, where people are dissatisfied in the organization and so on, rather than metrics like how long employees spend in the bathroom.

- The idea is to help individuals and the company as a whole perform better, not to punish individuals who aren't performing well. If someone isn't performing a task as well as expected, there may be a very good reason, such as fatigue or stress.

- The IoT and connected devices are playing an increasingly important role in driving employee performance. (Remember, connected workers are generally happier and more productive.) Likewise, AI is being used to create a more objective approach to performance management, and even predict performance.

- In today's fast-paced, technology-driven workplaces, annual performance appraisals just aren't working any more. Companies are moving away from annual reviews, and instead are generating more regular discussions and looking to the future more.

- It's really important to find a balance between monitoring employees and treating them like trusted adults. You want to enable performance, not micromanage or control people. Follow my best practice tips for using performance data in a fair, ethical way.

When it comes to enabling performance, we can't ignore the importance of training and developing your people. So, in the next chapter, let's explore how data and AI can help you provide a better learning experience for employees – and prepare the organization for the future.

Notes

1　E Singer. Extra sleep boosts basketball players' prowess, MIT Technology Review, 7 July 2011. www.technologyreview.com/2011/07/07/193127/extra-sleep-boosts-basketball-players-prowess (archived at https://perma.cc/4TBE-A4QK)

2　H James Wilson. Wearables in the workplace, *Harvard Business Review*, September 2013. hbr.org/2013/09/wearables-in-the-workplace (archived at https://perma.cc/748X-TP36)

3　S Frankel. Employers are using workplace wearables to find out how happy and productive we are, Quartz, 11 August 2016. qz.com/754989/employers-are-using-workplace-wearables-to-find-out-how-happy-and-productive-we-are (archived at https://perma.cc/T5AP-442V)

4　Accenture. Airbus soars with wearables, Accenture, nd. www.accenture.com/bg-en/case-studies/aerospace-defense/airbus-wearable-technology (archived at https://perma.cc/A3LD-HZWW)

5　T Greenwald. How AI is transforming the workplace, *The Wall Street Journal*, 12 March 2017. www.wsj.com/articles/how-ai-is-transforming-the-workplace-1489371060 (archived at https://perma.cc/5549-K5Y4)

6　B Marr. The future of performance management: How AI and big data combat workplace bias, Forbes, 17 January 2017. www.forbes.com/sites/bernardmarr/2017/01/17/the-future-of-performance-management-how-ai-and-big-data-combat-workplace-bias (archived at https://perma.cc/8MVR-E9MV)

7　S Shekhawat. Bots and artificial intelligence – next wave of disruption in HR, Your Story, 15 December 2016. yourstory.com/2016/12/bots-artificial-intelligence-hr (archived at https://perma.cc/AT8Y-V6NB)

8　S Garr. Performance management is broken, Deloitte, 5 March 2014. www2.deloitte.com/us/en/insights/focus/human-capital-trends/2014/hc-trends-2014-performance-management.html (archived at https://perma.cc/XPL8-E4NP)

9　J McGregor. What if you could replace performance evaluations with four simple questions? *The Washington Post*, 17 March 2015. www.washingtonpost.com/news/on-leadership/wp/2015/03/17/deloitte-ditches-performance-rankings-and-instead-will-ask-four-simple-questions (archived at https://perma.cc/G59E-6CX4)

10　K Snyder. We asked ChatGPT to write performance reviews and they are wildly sexist (and racist), Fast Company, 2 March 2023. www.fastcompany.com/90844066/chatgpt-write-performance-reviews-sexist-and-racist (archived at https://perma.cc/4KE5-FKGC)

11　M Ledwith. Tagged by their bosses, zero-hour Amazon workers, *Daily Mail*, 2 August 2013. www.dailymail.co.uk/news/article-2382800/Tagged-bosses-zero-hour-Amazon-workers-Employees-guaranteed-income.html (archived at https://perma.cc/7TCB-ZS3L)

12 J Kantor and D Stretifield. Inside Amazon: Wrestling big ideas in a bruising workplace, *The New York Times*, 16 August 2015. www.nytimes.com/2015/08/16/technology/inside-amazon-wrestling-big-ideas-in-a-bruising-workplace.html (archived at https://perma.cc/7UJA-9MRY)

13 Payscale. Companies with the most and least loyal employees, Payscale, nd. www.payscale.com/data-packages/employee-loyalty/least-loyal-employees (archived at https://perma.cc/RE8D-8QGH)

14 J Cook. Jeff Bezos responds to brutal NYT story, says it doesn't represent the Amazon he leads, GeekWire, 16 August 2015. www.geekwire.com/2015/full-memo-jeff-bezos-responds-to-cutting-nyt-expose-says-tolerance-for-lack-of-empathy-needs-to-be-zero (archived at https://perma.cc/5V8G-JJWT)

15 J Goldstein. The future of work looks like a UPS truck, NPR, 8 June 2016. www.npr.org/transcripts/481295201 (archived at https://perma.cc/DAW4-EKKL)

16 B Marr. Five inspiring ways organizations are using HR data, Forbes, 11 May 2018. www.forbes.com/sites/bernardmarr/2018/05/11/5-inspiring-ways-organizations-are-using-hr-data (archived at https://perma.cc/C95S-KYBZ)

17 J Goldstein. To increase productivity, UPS monitors drivers' every move, NPR,; 11 May 2018. www.npr.org/sections/money/2014/04/17/303770907/to-increase-productivity-ups-monitors-drivers-every-move (archived at https://perma.cc/4QSV-2KQG)

18 *The New York Times*. The rise of workplace surveillance, *The New York Times*, 24 August 2022. www.nytimes.com/2022/08/24/podcasts/the-daily/workplace-surveillance-productivity-tracking.html (archived at https://perma.cc/2Y8F-9Q8R)

19 J Waterson. *Daily Telegraph* installs workplace monitors on journalists' desks, Buzzfeed, 11 January 2016. www.buzzfeed.com/jimwaterson/telegraph-workplace-sensors (archived at https://perma.cc/Z2XP-LRDN)

20 Deloitte. Workplace burnout survey, Deloitte, 2015. www2.deloitte.com/us/en/pages/about-deloitte/articles/burnout-survey.html (archived at https://perma.cc/AZ77-9EGX)

21 K Morgan and D Nolan. How worker surveillance is backfiring on employers, BBC, 30 January 2023. www.bbc.com/worklife/article/20230127-how-worker-surveillance-is-backfiring-on-employers (archived at https://perma.cc/L2TH-QC6Z)

Data-driven employee training and development

10

A quick glimpse at the digital transformation happening in the world of education, particularly since the pandemic, shows us how technology can facilitate learning at all levels, from schools and universities to corporate learning. Today, everything in education can be measured, from how well a student performs in tests, to how well they engage with and understand the pages in an online course. For example, data has been used extensively in education, even in primary schools, to give a better understanding of skill levels, thereby helping to identify those who may be struggling and need extra support.

Developments like this can feed into a corporate training and development programme that is intelligently designed around the employees' and the organization's needs. An approach to learning that's better suited to today's rapidly changing workplace, where skills quickly become outdated and more tasks become automated. In this era of rapid transformation, upskilling and reskilling the workplace will become an even more critical part of what HR teams do. It's up to HR teams to ensure the workforce stays relevant, and that the organization finds the right balance between machine skills and human skills. This will be especially important as new advances like artificial intelligence and the metaverse play a larger role in the world of work.

Preparing the workforce for this data-driven, intelligent future is certainly a challenge for HR teams – but, as we'll see in this chapter, data and AI can be used to optimize employee training and development programmes, providing HR teams with insights into employee learning needs and preferences. By leveraging data and AI, organizations can create more effective and engaging training programmes, enhance employee skills and competencies and ultimately drive better business outcomes.

How data and AI are positively disrupting the education sector

I started this chapter by saying organizations can learn a lot from the data-driven revolution taking place in schools and universities. So let's explore some of these changes.

With more learning now coordinated online and often taking place via a laptop or tablet, even when the student is in a traditional classroom environment, increasingly large amounts of data are being generated about how students learn. Innovators working with educational establishments are turning this data into insights that can identify better teaching strategies, highlight areas where students may not be learning efficiently and transform the delivery of education.

Learning that's tailored to individual students

Education has always fundamentally been about feedback loops. A teacher presents a problem and the student attempts to solve it. From that attempt, the teacher can learn what the student understands and doesn't understand, and can adjust his or her instruction accordingly. Likewise, the student understands more about the problem he or she attempted. When a teacher is faced with a classroom overflowing with students, data and AI help to facilitate this feedback process.

Any teacher can walk students through a course. But to pinpoint and develop the specific problem areas of each student in a classroom of many is a tough undertaking. This is why numerous adaptive learning companies like Knewton have sprung up, offering services that analyse the progress of students, from the nursery class to university level, to create better test questions and personalized learning materials. Crucially, these data-driven courses adapt to each individual student. Technology now makes it possible to assess, in real time, whether a section is too easy, too hard, or just right for that student, and adjust the remaining course materials accordingly.

Personalized learning like this also allows students to learn at their own pace, regardless of what the other students around them are doing. Then, the teacher can receive that information and understand where any one student might be struggling, or analyse the performance of a class as a whole.

The impact of AI in schools

The best teachers go into the profession because they're passionate about educating young people and they thrive on seeing a student's eyes light up when they understand a subject. The idea of effectively becoming a data administrator may not appeal to most teachers. It's the classic human vs. machine scenario: as AI gets better at teaching and providing educational assistance, the question inevitably turns to whether human teachers will be replaced by computers.

Now, I don't believe cyborgs are going to take over our classrooms. Instead, teachers and AI systems will team up to provide stronger, better educational experiences for students at every level. Here are just some of the ways AI is positively disrupting education:

- AI can automate basic, repetitive activities like marking multiple-choice papers and grading fill-in-the-blank-style homework.

- Educational programmes can adjust the speed at which individual students go through coursework, provide additional help when a student is getting stuck, or provide additional enrichment when a student is working ahead of the rest of the class.

- AI can help the teacher provide better learning experiences. For example, if the software notes that a large percentage of students are missing a particular question, it can provide important feedback to the teacher that his or her lesson may need additional details.

- AI systems can provide valuable feedback to parents, educators and administrators. This could reduce the need for separate standardized testing and provide a level playing field for helping to assess teacher and school performance.

Real-world examples from the education sector

There are numerous examples of how technology is helping both teachers and students get the most out of their school days. In Wisconsin's Menomonee Falls School District, for example, data has been put to use for everything from improving classroom cleanliness to planning school bus routes, after department leaders were encouraged to attend classes themselves on how to gain insights from data and analytics.[1]

Data has also been used to help improve student behaviour. One US middle school found that, for some reason, the number of pupils being sent to the principal's office for disciplinary reasons had grown by a worrying amount. On examining the data, they realized that this had coincided with a reduction in school excursions such as ice skating and sledding trips. When these were reinstated, behaviour among students improved, leading to a noticeable reduction in the number being sent to see the principal.[2]

Schools are also finding themselves armed with new technologies aimed at cutting down on exam cheating and plagiarism among students. The Proctortrack system aims to prevent cheating by using webcams and microphones to monitor students while they sit for online exams. By building profiles of cheating behaviour, it is able to recognize and flag suspicious activity. Proctortrack also uses facial recognition to ensure that the correct student is taking the test, monitors computer activity to make sure that unauthorized sources aren't being consulted, and even tracks eyeball movement during the assessment. The system can be used for tests taking place in traditional exam room environments as well as remote learning.

Of course, not all education takes place in the first two decades of life or in a traditional classroom setting. Online courses mean people of all ages can grow their skills and knowledge, regardless of their geographical location, income level and other factors. These massive open online courses (MOOCs) – which deliver all of the learning materials and exams via a computer or tablet – are providing a wealth of insights into the ways that people learn.

As we'll see in this chapter, trends from the education sector – such as the ability to deliver more personalized learning, and to track learners' progress – are now filtering into the world of workplace learning. But before you can optimize your workplace learning offering, you may first need to identify where there are skills gaps in your organization.

What skills does your organization need?

We know from Chapter 9 that data can significantly improve a company's ability to assess performance and pinpoint exactly where employees are performing well and where they may need some extra assistance. In this way, data helps HR teams identify gaps in learning, so that they can plug those gaps through appropriate training.

Clearly, with data, analytics and automation developing at the pace they are, and with no sign of that exhausting pace letting up, one major function of HR is to help fill the digital skills gap. HR teams have a responsibility to ensure more people in the organization have the necessary skills to prepare for the data-driven transformation of business. There's no doubt in my mind that the ability to tap into and nurture digital skills is going to be critical to most businesses' success in the future. Yet, more than 12 million employees in the UK do not have the necessary digital skills.[3]

That said, the key skills for success aren't just centred around digital skills. Far from it. Certainly, digital skills will be important for the workforce, but it would be a mistake to overlook the importance of soft skills. The things that machines can't do, basically.

In my book *Future Skills: The 20 skills and competencies everyone needs to succeed in a digital world* I set out the skills that I believe will help organizations – and individuals – surf the wave of digital transformation. I'll briefly summarize those skills below.

The essential future skills are:

Essential future skills

1   *Digital literacy:* The digital skills needed to learn, work and navigate everyday life, including using devices, software and apps with confidence; communicating and collaborating via digital tools; and keeping abreast of new technologies.

2   *Data literacy:* Being able to access appropriate data, work with data confidently (creating/gathering data, keeping it up to date, etc.), extract meaning from data and communicate those data-based insights to others.

3   *Technical skills:* The huge variety of 'hard' skills that are necessary for many jobs (such as accountancy skills for accountants, coding skills for software developers, and so on).

4   *Digital threat awareness:* Being aware of the dangers of being online or using digital devices, including hacking, phishing, privacy violations, cyberbullying, digital addiction, etc. And knowing how to keep yourself (and your organization) safe.

5   *Critical thinking:* The ability to think objectively, and to analyse issues or situations based on evidence rather than personal opinions or biases.

6   *Judgement and complex decision making:* For me, the ability to make sound decisions also includes recognizing the impact that personal preferences, values and beliefs have on our judgement.

7   *Emotional intelligence and empathy:* So long as there are humans in the workplace and human-to-human relationships, we will need emotional intelligence (the ability to be aware of, express and control our emotions) and empathy (the ability to see the world from someone else's perspective).

8   *Creativity:* The act of turning imaginative ideas into reality absolutely belongs in the workplace, especially as we give more and more routine tasks over to machines. Creativity enables creative thinking and problem solving.

9   *Collaboration and working in teams:* As the nature of collaboration and teamwork evolves to include hybrid workers, fully remote workers and gig workers, we will need collaborative skills more than ever.

10 *Interpersonal communication:* Communication in all its forms (oral, written, non-verbal and, importantly, listening) remains a vital skill for workplace success.

11 *Working in gigs:* Because we must all prepare for a future in which more people work as 'free agents'.

12 *Adaptability and flexibility:* In the workplaces of the future, change is going to be even more of a driving factor than it is today. We must therefore all develop the mental resilience to thrive amidst constant change.

13 *Cultural intelligence and diversity consciousness:* Which means incorporating a basic awareness of diversity (and the recognition that diversity is a good thing), and the ability to relate to others from different backgrounds.

14 *Ethical awareness:* Because digital transformation has given rise to a whole new set of ethical challenges to overcome (such as the dilemmas surrounding artificial intelligence or the use of people's personal data).

15 *Leadership skills:* The combination of factors that will shape 21st-century work – distributed teams, increasing diversity, humans transitioning to more creative tasks, the gig economy, fluid organizational structures, and so on – means that leadership skills will be important not just for traditional leadership roles, but for a wide range of roles across the organization.

16 *Brand of 'you' and networking:* The ability to build and maintain a personal brand, establish your expertise, grow your network, make new connections and enhance your career.

17 *Time management:* By which I mean the ability to work smarter rather than working longer or harder.

18 *Curiosity and continuous learning:* One of the most important skills on the list (if not the most important). Because curiosity and continual learning is fundamental to being able (and willing) to embrace change. Which brings me to…

19 *Embracing and celebrating change:* I've already mentioned adaptability (the mental resilience to thrive amidst change) on this list, but individuals and organizations will also need the practical skills to embrace and manage change successfully.

20 *Looking after yourself:* By which I mean creating a more balanced life, and taking good care of your mental and physical health.

Do keep these skills in mind as you read this chapter, and consider how your organization can build and maintain them. But also keep in mind that the jobs that people do will undoubtedly change in the future – many jobs will evolve, many will become obsolete, and many new jobs will emerge. So when you think about the essential skills that will drive your company forward, try to consider not just the jobs that exist today in your organization, but also the sorts of jobs that may exist in the future.

The major trends in data-driven workplace learning

Workplace learning is moving away from traditional models where participants go to a specific place for a set duration of time to learn at a pre-defined pace. Now, for workers, learning is becoming something to dip into much more frequently, perhaps in more bite-size pieces, and at their own pace. Learning is essentially becoming a core part of the day-to-day job – a more continual approach to learning than we've seen in the past.

So how can data and AI aid this process? By leveraging data from various sources such as employee performance data, surveys and feedback,

AI algorithms can identify knowledge gaps and recommend personalized training programmes that align with employees' learning styles and career goals. AI-powered learning platforms can also provide employees with real-time feedback and coaching, creating a more engaging and interactive learning experience. What's more, data and AI can be used to measure the impact and effectiveness of training programmes, allowing HR teams to continuously improve and optimize their learning and development initiatives.

Learning that's adapted to individual employees

Thanks to online learning, data and analytics, training and development is becoming increasingly personalized to individual learners. 'Adaptive' learning technology allows courses, segments of courses, activities and test questions to be personalized to suit the learner's preference, pace of learning and best way of learning. As well as allowing individuals to learn at their own pace, online learning also offers the same big advantage seen in the education sector: the ability to measure how individual participants are progressing, how well they're retaining the information and where additional guidance or information might be required. Individual, self-paced online learning is also arguably more cost effective than pulling employees out of their job for a day or week to send them on expensive training courses. Self-directed learning like this also helps integrate ongoing development into workers' everyday routines. Danone's online Campus X is one example of this in action. The food giant has created a user-friendly online platform where employees can boost their development and share best practice and knowledge with other staff.

The use of AI in personalized learning

Online learning allows for much greater measurement, because learners leave behind digital traces of everything they do within the parameters of the course they're taking – and these traces include how quickly the learner moved through a particular element of the course, where they paused, where they got a test question wrong, which material they revisited and even, potentially, what time of day the learner best assimilates information. Learning management systems allow providers to track this data and use those insights to tailor courses to individuals' needs and, therefore, make them much more engaging.

AI is critical in this ability to provide adaptive, personalized learning. It is AI (particularly machine learning) that allows providers to identify where a learner might be struggling and what areas need extra emphasis for that individual. Analytics company Zoomi, for example, uses AI capabilities to analyse each learner's behaviour, performance, engagement and comprehension to improve learning content and create a uniquely individual learning experience. Zoomi claims its solution can increase knowledge transfer by 50 per cent and improve business outcomes by 60 per cent.[4]

The evidence for an AI-based approach is clear. One paper published by Pearson and UCL set out how AI creates learning programmes that are more flexible, efficient and inclusive.[5] In particular, the authors cited how AI effectively allows personalized, one-on-one learning to be provided on a large scale, which is especially beneficial for larger companies with a diverse network of employees with different training needs.

Naturally, this works both ways. Not only can personalized learning track how individuals are progressing, it also allows learners to provide instant feedback on course content and features.

Micro, mobile and blended learning

Building on the idea of employees learning when it best suits them, 'micro learning' has become a bit of a buzz phrase in training. Micro learning involves very short bursts of learning, often delivered through short videos of just a couple of minutes. These are typically delivered as part of a wider course, and are used to help learners absorb information more quickly and easily. We all know how information is easier to absorb in small chunks at a time rather than in one massive deluge. Micro learning capitalizes on this.

Mobile learning is another trend in learning and development, as more and more providers support mobile devices in their programmes. Mobile access to learning content allows employees the flexibility to learn when and where it suits them, for example when there are few distractions around. It also fits with the increase in remote working.

Finally, 'blended learning', a phrase commonly used to describe the marriage of online learning and classroom learning, is proving very popular as companies transition away from traditional training models. So what works for your company may indeed be a blend of traditional training courses and self-directed learning.

Remote learning and the virtual classroom

One of my favourite examples of just how much learning has transformed comes from Harvard Business School (HBS), which created a digital class-room as a template of the classroom of the future.[6] In this virtual classroom, the lecturer teaches in a specially designed broadcast studio. Cameras follow the lecturer as they address a huge screen made up of faces – live-feed videos (with audio) of all the students participating in the lecture, connected to the class simply by their laptops. This virtual classroom, which HBS has called HBX Live, took three years of planning and development, and is designed to integrate seamlessly with HBS's online teaching programmes.

One thing that's really striking about this virtual classroom is the extent to which it feels like a real classroom experience to the lecturer and students participating. The system was designed so that all microphones would be on all the time, including the students', and no one was muted. This makes for a much more collaborative, authentic learning experience, where students can laugh along if the professor makes a joke and agree verbally when some-one makes a good point. When a student wants to interject with a question or point, rather than raising their hands, they simply click a button on their computer and their nameplate on the screen turns red, letting the lecturer know that they have something to say. Students can also type comments via a chat bar, and the comments then scroll along the bottom of the huge video screen like a news ticker. And, even more impressive, up to 60 students can participate in these virtual classes at a time, which is quite a feat when you consider that's 60 separate video feeds being managed in real time without any delay. The system also allows for up to 1,000 additional students to observe the virtual lesson with a time delay. In the future, we could see em-ployers develop their own version of the Harvard classroom – or, of course, tap into services provided by forward-thinking schools like Harvard. There's a great example from Walmart coming up later in the chapter.

What's more, some providers are going a step further to create immersive courses that incorporate virtual reality and augmented reality (AR). But we'll talk more about that later in the chapter.

Making use of MOOCs

Because of their vastness ('massive' being the big clue in the name), MOOCs provide a unique opportunity for data. Huge amounts of data can be gath-ered both on individuals but also across multiple learners to pick up broader patterns and insights. These courses allow providers to map an individual's learning trajectory, identify trouble spots and provide targeted interventions where needed.

MOOCs from the likes of Coursera and Khan Academy provide accessible learning opportunities for millions of people around the world, covering anything from vocational learning to degree-level courses. In MOOCs, learners undertake self-directed learning when it suits them, engage with bite-size micro-learning content like short videos and participate in collaborative discussions with other learners.

Today, many corporate learning programmes are making use of MOOCs to deliver training to their employees. Companies like Microsoft are creating their own custom MOOCs for employees. Global steel manufacturer Tenaris has created MOOCs on various topics, including technical topics like 'Introduction to steel'. Tenaris is now offering the MOOCs externally to attract university students and boost its employer brand. Other organizations, such as Bank of America, are leveraging content from existing MOOCs to deliver training on core competencies. This strategy allows businesses of all sizes to curate a wide range of content that suits their needs in a simple, cost-effective way. Both strategies are innovative ways of rethinking your learning offering and capitalizing on the latest advances in learning technology.

Measuring how learners are doing – and how effective your training is

When learners work through the content in a digital course, they leave a digital trace of all their actions. This ability to track learners' journeys gives training providers and HR professionals the opportunity to understand a great deal about the learning experience. Indeed, most learning providers incorporate some sort of learning management system that tracks how learners progress and provides insights that can help both individual learners and the company-wide education programme.

Learning analytics should therefore underpin every aspect of employee learning, from developing better learning programmes, to delivering them in the most engaging way, to tracking how employees interact with the training. Data and analytics can also dramatically improve the measurement of your training offering by showing how effective (or not) it is in practice. Typically, the effectiveness of corporate training is assessed by employees filling out a basic evaluation questionnaire after the course. But data allows us to go so much further, and pinpoint exactly what's working and what isn't. Two specific data points that every company should be measuring are employee comprehension (e.g. are people struggling with various aspects of the content?), and employee engagement with content (e.g. are they taking up opportunities for learning, and are they then participating in courses all the way through or are they ignoring various aspects?).

Data also allows HR teams to create clear, evidence-based links between training and performance, which is helpful for improving future training and development, establishing ROI, and securing leadership buy-in for training programmes.

The cutting edge: Incorporating VR, AR, digital twins and the metaverse

Interestingly, VR and AR are becoming more common tools in corporate learning – in particular, many vendors are now offering VR- and AR-enabled training programmes. Beyond that, digital twin technology and the metaverse may play an increasingly important role.

Let's explore the cutting edge of workplace learning.

Using VR to create immersive training scenarios

VR creates an interactive environment by generating realistic images, sounds and other sensations to fully immerse the user in that environment. It's easy to imagine how this technology could be used to provide immersive training experiences in fields as diverse as medicine, the armed forces, engineering and many more. This isn't a new idea – just think of flight simulators, for example – but the ever-decreasing cost of VR hardware (headsets, gloves, etc.) has made the technology more accessible to a far wider audience. VR technology can even be used on smartphones, although that tends to be less immersive than using a VR headset.

VR brings enormous benefits to workplace learning because it allows learners to learn by *doing* and *seeing*. And, for most of us, learning by doing or seeing is a much better way of understanding and retaining information compared to, say, listening to a trainer explain a concept, or reading information onscreen in a PowerPoint presentation. In particular, VR has huge potential when it comes to training for scenarios that are too difficult, dangerous or expensive to recreate in real life – such as firefighter and law enforcement training.

BP is one company that's invested in VR-enabled training for employees working in dangerous situations. To train employees in start-up and emergency exit procedures at BP's oil refinery in Hull, UK, the company partnered with Igloo Vision – known for creating immersive shared VR spaces. When you work in an oil refinery, mistakes can be fatal, but this virtual training allowed employees to learn from their mistakes safely. How they pulled off this training is particularly interesting; rather than trainees each wearing their own VR headset, Igloo Vision built a six-meter igloo at the Hull refinery.[7] Inside the igloo, employees could experience an extremely detailed replica of the plant and practise critical safety tasks, all in a safe virtual setting. What's great about this is it provides the opportunity to assess whole shift teams at a time, rather than immersing each individual in their own simulation. This could be the future of critical team-based training exercises and assessments.

But it's not just high-risk jobs that benefit from VR training. Athletes are also beginning to make greater use of this technology. Any sports training regimen relies on repetition, whether it's on a football field, tennis court or wherever. But getting those reps in can be a challenge – particularly if the weather is bad, or you're travelling, or even injured. Immersive learning specialists Strivr set out to change all that with their immersive learning technology. Although the technology was originally developed for sports teams, Strivr now works with a wide range of corporate partners to deliver immersive enterprise learning – including companies like Verizon, MGM Resorts, Sprouts, JetBlue and Stanford Children's Hospital.

One Strivr partner is Walmart. And when the US's largest employer gets behind VR training, you know other organizations are bound to follow suit. Walmart is using VR to train associates and the next generation of managers via its Walmart Academy. Originally, the Walmart Academy comprised physical classrooms in stores around the US. But now, thanks to its partnership with Strivr, training can be efficiently delivered to Walmart employees around the world. Employees can access the training via VR headsets and iPads (provided for training purposes in Walmart stores) or by using the Walmart Academy app, which is great for bite-size on-demand training sessions. This VR-enabled evolution of the Walmart Academy will deliver job-specific training, future skills training, wellness courses and leadership training. Walmart first began using VR-based training in 2018, so it is no stranger to the technology, and the company reports that VR has helped Walmart employees 'feel more confident and prepared to perform their job'.[8] Interestingly, Walmart also offers immersive classes via video conferencing, using software that's similar to the Harvard virtual classroom I mentioned earlier in the chapter.

Clearly, VR can play a key role in a variety of job-specific training. But even soft business skills can be learned with VR technology. As an example, VirtualSpeech's app makes use of Google Cardboard VR smartphone technology to allow users to practise their public speaking and interpersonal communication skills. Combining practical experience, online reading materials and videos that teach basic skills, and instant feedback, the course aims to help people develop quickly and build their confidence in a safe environment. It's easy to see how VR technology like this could be incorporated into training and development programmes to boost employees' presentation skills.

It's reality, Jim, but not as we know it – tapping into AR

While VR plunges the user into a simulated world, AR is rooted firmly in reality, and adds an extra layer of information to the real world that the user sees in front of them. Basically, AR is used to project digital elements – such as text or images – onto the real world around us, just as the Pokémon GO mobile game projects Pokémon characters onto the real world via your phone camera. AR is also referred to as *mixed reality* or *hybrid reality*. Typically, AR is used with a simple smartphone, but there are also specific AR glasses and headsets available, such as Google Glass and the HoloLens headset.

Even though it is less immersive, AR still bring many advantages to workplace learning. In one example, multinational engineering conglomerate Honeywell has been using AR to address the problem of knowledge 'leakage', where older workers retire and take their knowledge with them. Traditionally, retirees were asked to put their knowledge into PowerPoint slides or Word documents that could be shared in classroom-like spaces with new hires. But Honeywell found that this passive learning experience led to an information retention rate of just 20–30 per cent. So they equipped both departing workers and new hires with a HoloLens mixed reality headset, allowing retirees to record exactly what they were doing in their work so that new workers could see this information overlaid onto their own work activities in front of them. This more active form of training boosted the level of information retained from 30 per cent (at best) to 80 per cent.[9] How impressive is that?

Creating digital twins

Digital twin technology is closely related to AR because it pairs the virtual and physical worlds. Quite simply, a digital twin is a digital model of a process, product or service that allows analysis of data and monitoring of systems to identify problems before they even occur, prevent downtime and even plan for the future by using simulations.

How do digital twins work? First, smart components that use sensors to gather data about real-time status, working condition or position are integrated with a physical item (such as a factory machine). The components are connected to a cloud-based system that receives and processes all the data the sensors monitor. This input is then analysed, and lessons are learned and opportunities are uncovered within the virtual environment that can be applied to the physical world. One example of this in action comes from General Electric's (GE's) 'digital wind farm'. GE uses digital twin technology to inform the configuration of each wind turbine prior to construction in order to generate efficiency gains.[10]

While digital twins are largely used to drive performance and efficiency, it's not a huge leap to imagine how this technology could be used to enhance training for a wide range of employees, particularly in the field of engineering.

Using the metaverse in your training

Virtual reality, augmented reality and digital twin technologies are all closely related to – and enablers of – the metaverse. So it's fair to expect the metaverse will play a part in workplace learning in future. After all, the metaverse is all about creating immersive experiences and environments, usually accessed through VR or AR technologies. So the next step in VR- and AR-enabled training may involve employers delivering immersive training sessions in their own little corner of metaverse.

Indeed, providers are already emerging that provide metaverse training offerings. One example is Virbela, which offers a platform for virtual classrooms, allowing learners and teachers to interact in a virtual, 3D, immersive space. Another option for metaverse training is immersive simulations of specific scenarios. If you think about it, in the metaverse, you could create whatever training scenarios you wanted – such as customer service training in a virtual store with virtual customers, or engineering training that takes the user 'inside' the workings of a machine or component. Medical training is already moving in this direction with platforms like Fundamental Surgery, which allows medical professionals to practise surgical procedures virtually. There are also platforms that provide immersive virtual spaces for companies to host their team-building events (one example being Teamflow). Solutions like this are great when you want to bring team members who are scattered in multiple locations together in one place, without the time and expense associated with travel. The metaverse also allows great scope for gamification, with companies like Classcraft creating learning experiences that provide students with interactive games and challenges.

CASE STUDY   Even more cutting edge: The use of generative AI in training and development

Another cutting-edge area of workplace learning and development involves using generative AI to automatically create educational content. From written text and videos to interactive quizzes, generative AI tools (such as the GPT chatbot we've already mentioned in this book) can be used to create a wide range of educational content – saving trainers a lot of time and effort. (And saving cost, especially if you currently outsource your content creation.)

It's now possible, for example, to convert a video lecture or podcast into written course content through AI. Conversely, your written content can easily be converted into videos, complete with virtual presenters, thanks to tools like Synthesia. This content can be incredibly realistic and engaging. Take it from me – because I use Synthesia's generative AI tool to create my own video content. I simply write a script and the tool turns my text into a video featuring my virtual avatar (I call him 'Bernard Marr 2.0'). This allows me to create videos incredibly quickly, without the hassle of setting up cameras, recording myself and editing footage.

You don't have to create an avatar of yourself, if that doesn't appeal. Synthesia has over 100 stock avatar presenters for you to choose from (great for ensuring your videos are diverse and inclusive). And you can type your text in over 120 languages. Synthesia reckons its tool has saved companies $5,000 per video versus traditional course creation methods, helped cut video production time by 50 per cent and helped employers increase engagement by over 30 per cent.[11]

Already, the Synthesia tool is very impressive. But it's also important to re-member that technology like this will only get better and better in future, allowing employers to create even more immersive and engaging learning materials, quickly and easily. Boring PowerPoint training sessions might soon be a quaint thing of the past!

But what else can generative AI do besides generating course content? Well, generative AI tools can help you design and structure course content – which is great when you're developing a new training course from scratch. And, of course, the AI element means learning can be highly personalized to individual learners, if required.

AI-powered chatbots can also provide learners with round-the-clock support, answering questions they may have as they complete courses. Many questions are common across all learners, so it makes sense that chatbots could handle these FAQs. It's a bit like having a personalized digital tutor on hand at every stage of learning.

Established learning providers are already using generative AI to enhance and create educational content. One example comes from language learning app Duolingo, which is using Open AI's GPT-4 generative AI tool to deliver a more personalized experience to language learners.

Already a pioneer in AI-enhanced education, Duolingo is using GPT-4 as part of its mission to create the ultimate virtual language tutor.[12] At the time of writing, the Duolingo app has harnessed GPT-4 in two ways: firstly, a role-playing feature that allows users to interact with an AI-powered persona and carry out various learning-focused tasks (for example, conversing with an AI barista in a Parisian café); and secondly, in a feature called 'Explain My Answer', which gives users a detailed, personalized explanation of why an answer they have given is correct or incorrect. Thanks to generative AI, Duolingo's app feels more like a human language tutor than ever. In the future, Duolingo aims to use GPT-4 to generate new course content, which has traditionally been a bottleneck area for the company.

Of course, as with other uses of AI, there are challenges in using generative AI – bias being a potential pitfall. What other challenges lie ahead for organizations using data and AI to enhance their training?

A quick look at the downsides of data-driven training and development

Naturally, there are ethical and practical concerns around working with individuals' learning data, particularly when it comes to data privacy and security. (Circle back to Chapter 4 for more on this.) Data breaches are always a legitimate concern, and rightly so. In one example, a school district in

Tennessee inadvertently left the names, addresses, birth dates and full social security numbers of 18,000 students on an unsecured server for months![13] Ensuring your employees' data is private and secure is a critical concern for any HR team. These days, it's incredibly naïve to think you don't have to worry about protecting your employees' data. Where possible, anonymizing employees' training-related data will help. Where anonymizing data isn't possible, you will need to ensure the data is kept secure.

Good practices of data minimization and transparency are also essential. There is no point in gathering data for data's sake. Therefore, if you don't intend to use training data to make improvements, then don't gather it. It's as simple as that. And when you do intend to gather it, make sure you're upfront with your employees about what information you're gathering and why. If it's clear this data is being analysed to help improve the delivery of learning programmes in the future, and to facilitate individuals' development within the company, staff are much more likely to get on board.

Key takeaways

We've covered a lot of ground in this chapter, so let's recap the main takeaways:

- Upskilling and reskilling the workforce – basically, preparing the organization for the intelligence revolution by developing future skills – is one of the most important and challenging jobs for HR teams in the future. Data and AI have a huge role to play in this.

- Workplace learning is undergoing a massive digital transformation, with key trends being adaptive and personalized learning, micro learning, remote and blended learning and MOOCs. Data and AI are also being used to track how employees engage with training programmes.

- VR and AR are becoming more common tools in workplace learning, allowing employers to simulate a wide range of scenarios and deliver a more immersive, engaging training experience. We can also expect the metaverse to play an increasing role in training and development.

- And at the very cutting edge, generative AI is being used to automatically generate course content and support learners' needs. A good example is using generative AI to create video content.

- Do ensure you take necessary steps to protect your employees' learning data and minimize data collection wherever possible.

Now let's turn to the final chapter in this part and see how data and AI can improve the work of HR in ensuring employee safety and wellbeing.

Notes

1   M Rich. Some schools embrace demands for education data, *The New York Times*, 11 May 2015. www.nytimes.com/2015/05/12/us/school-districts-embrace-business-model-of-data-collection.html (archived at https://perma.cc/84HS-8588)

2   K Pal. How big data can revolutionize education, Techopedia, 1 May 2018. www.techopedia.com/2/31725/trends/how-big-data-can-revolutionize-education (archived at https://perma.cc/Y86U-SXVE)

3   R Cellan-Jones. More than 12 million fall into UK digital skills gap, BBC News, 19 October 2015. www.bbc.com/news/technology-34570344 (archived at https://perma.cc/2PC5-6BZA)

4   Zoomi. Next generation learning, Zoomi, nd. zoomi.ai/next-generation-learning (archived at https://perma.cc/V9SH-8CTX)

5   UCL. Why we should take artificial intelligence in education more seriously, UCL, 13 April 2016. www.ucl.ac.uk/ioe/news-events/news-pub/april-2016/New-paper-published-by-pearson-makes-the-case-for-why-we-must-take-artificial-intelligence-in-education-more-seriously (archived at https://perma.cc/9RVQ-LJY8)

6   J A Byrne. Harvard Business School really has created the classroom of the future, Fortune, 25 August 2015. fortune.com/2015/08/25/harvard-business-school-hbx (archived at https://perma.cc/7YRG-TCMQ)

7   Igloo Vision. BP training, Igloo Vision, nd. www.igloovision.com/case-studies/bp-training (archived at https://perma.cc/AQ79-GKXY)

8   P Albinus. What HR tech is behind Walmart's new Global Upskilling Academy? HR Executive, 9 June 2022. hrexecutive.com/what-hr-tech-is-behind-walmarts-new-global-upskilling-academy (archived at https://perma.cc/NL33-E9XT)

9   B Marr. The amazing ways Honeywell is using virtual and augmented reality to transfer skills to millennials, Forbes, 7 March 2018. www.forbes.com/sites/bernardmarr/2018/03/07/the-amazing-ways-honeywell-is-using-virtual-and-augmented-reality-to-transfer-skills-to-millennials (archived at https://perma.cc/T8JS-BQM4)

10 GE. Meet the digital wind farm, GE, nd. www.ge.com/renewableenergy/stories/meet-the-digital-wind-farm (archived at https://perma.cc/9P4R-P9DB)

11 Synthesia. www.synthesia.io (archived at https://perma.cc/L8ET-5KAA)

12 B Marr. The amazing ways Duolingo is using AI and GPT-4, Forbes, 28 April
    2023. www.forbes.com/sites/bernardmarr/2023/04/28/the-amazing-ways-
    duolingo-is-using-ai-and-gpt-4 (archived at https://perma.cc/BKM7-3TZ8)

13 B Marr. Big data in the classroom, LinkedIn, 31 July 2014. www.linkedin.com/
    pulse/20140731081214-64875646-big-data-in-the-classroom-why-learning-
    will-never-be-the-same (archived at https://perma.cc/2RQF-JNWD)

Employee safety and wellbeing 11

Employee safety and wellbeing are critical areas of any HR team's work. Intelligent, data-driven HR is about using data and AI to better manage employee safety and boost employee wellbeing and wellness. Technology, and particularly sensors, has helped to make the work environment safer for a long time now – think smoke alarms, gas sensors, security and entry systems and the like – but as we'll see in this chapter, the emergence of data- and AI-driven tools has taken this to a completely new level.

By leveraging data from various sources, such as wearable devices and environmental sensors, AI algorithms can provide real-time insights into employee health and safety, identifying potential hazards and providing personalized recommendations for prevention. And thanks to developments in virtual reality and the metaverse, employers can now create more immersive and engaging virtual experiences that help employees to identify and manage potential risks and improve their overall wellbeing. By using data, AI and the metaverse in this way, organizations can create a more proactive, immersive and personalized approach to employee safety and wellbeing, enhancing employee engagement, retention and overall quality of life.

Improving employee safety with data and analytics

Making sure people are safe at work is a critically important role of data and AI. Obviously, there is a sliding scale of technology, from completely automated robotics-driven factories at one end of the scale, to the more realistic (for most businesses, at least) end of the scale where sensors and other technology are deployed as part of a health and safety programme. This chapter assumes that your business sits at the latter end of the scale, where humans and machines work together to improve employee safety.

Indeed, it's incredibly powerful when workplace systems are aware of the people in the workplace – what they're doing, how they're performing and how they're feeling – and this is perhaps one of the main driving forces in making our workplaces safer (and employees happier).

Embracing technology, not abdicating responsibility to technology

In this way, I'm not talking about companies handing all responsibility for employee safety over to machines. There was a Georgia Tech study a few years ago in which participants were found to trust safety robots over their own common sense – even when it was obvious the robot was leading them into a dangerous situation.[1] In the experiment, people were guided to a room by a clearly faulty robot; it either took them an obviously inefficient route to the room in question, or broke down in the process – all of which was set up by researcher. Once the participants were settled in the room, the smoke alarm was triggered and the unreliable robot then guided them through corridors filled with artificial smoke. Here's the scary part: even though the robot was clearly leading people the wrong way, away from emergency exit signs, most people in the study still chose to follow the robot. A few even followed the robot into a dark room blocked by furniture – again all set up by the researcher. People trusted the robot, despite the fact that it had proven itself faulty or unreliable at the start of the experiment. This crazy outcome shows how we need to marry technology with human experience and common sense, rather than just turn over all responsibility for our safety to machines.

In today's data-driven world, almost everything can be measured, and it's now possible for companies to measure a great deal about what their employees are doing and how they're feeling. The world of healthcare shows us just how much can be measured these days. Cloud-based health monitoring, which is at the cutting edge of modern medicine, enables healthcare professionals to monitor people's health from afar and provide help or advice when needed. Even the Apple Watch can monitor your heart health and perform an ECG. As we'll see in this chapter, wearable technologies can play a huge role in employee safety and wellbeing, and the technology is advancing all the time.

How the Internet of Things is making workplaces safer

Of course employers want their workplaces to be safe environments where no one gets hurt. Yet workplace accidents and work-related health issues remain a problem. In the UK, for example, the Health and Safety Executive reports that 565,000 workers sustained an injury at work in the year 2021–22, and that the cost of injuries and ill health due to working conditions is more than £18 billion.[2] The impact of work-related accidents and health problems is huge, both for the individuals and their families, but also for the employer in question and their reputation. Clearly, something needs to change.

Changing employee behaviour

In recent years, the IoT – smart devices, wearables and sensors that are connected to the internet – has transformed the way we think about and deliver employee safety. One of the challenges in workplace safety is getting employees to change their behaviour in line with existing company safety rules or to adopt new safety initiatives. And this can be particularly helpful in industries or companies that rely on contract or temporary employees, like construction. The IoT helps encourage employee adoption of safety initiatives by providing much clearer monitoring and insights into safety-related behaviour. IoT devices, particularly wearables but also sensors, can now generate a mountain of real-time data on workplace safety and employee activities. Not only can this data show whether safety rules and initiatives are being properly adopted, it can also lead to insights that help improve safety programmes in the future. And the more this data improves safety programmes, the greater employee buy-in is, and the more likely employees are to adopt new or improved safety initiatives in future.

Crucially, because IoT devices can be used to transmit real-time data for on-the-fly analysis, managers can then be alerted when unsafe practices are taking place and take appropriate action. For example, video data can be used to detect when an employee is not wearing the appropriate safety gear, prompting a notification to be sent to the employee's supervisor. Analytics like this can help to significantly reduce workplace accidents and injuries. Indeed, our ability to predict workplace accidents is improving all the time. Researchers at Carnegie Mellon University, for example, used real-world data to create predictive safety models with accuracy rates of between 80 and 97 per cent.[3] The model takes workplace safety inspection data and uses this to predict not just the number, but also the location of safety incidents over the next month.

The role of wearables

Wearable IoT devices, such as sensors, tracking bands and smart helmets, are now being used across a variety of industries. Clearly, wearable technology will have a huge impact on the field of employee safety, and the vision of a 'connected worker' is becoming reality in many different industries. The beauty of IoT devices is that they make employees (and their supervisors) more aware of what they're doing and the environment around them, whether that means alerting someone when they're close to over-exerting themselves and need to take a break, or raising the alarm when the proper safety equipment is not being used. This awareness in itself can dramatically improve safety, because more aware workers are likely to behave in a much more safety-conscious manner. What is really exciting is the ability not only to monitor individuals in real time, but also to personalize advice and actions to individuals based on what the data is telling us.

Sensor technology can also be used to monitor the environment that someone is working in. Data can be gathered on temperature, noise levels, humidity, light levels, toxic gases and radiation. Robots can effectively 'smell' now, and can use sensors to detect chemical signatures like blood or alcohol in the air. Blanca Lorena Villarreal, a researcher from the Tecnológico de Monterrey in Mexico, has developed an 'electronic nose' that can be built into robotic devices.[4] For me, there's no question that the IoT is the future of employee safety.

Making driving safer

Driving remains one of the most dangerous things humans do, whether it's simply driving to and from work, taking to the road to visit clients, or driving machinery as part of the job.

Driver fatigue is a huge issue that contributes to a significant portion of accidents. So if your employees are driving vehicles as part of their job, it pays to make sure they're not struggling due to fatigue. And this doesn't just apply to transportation companies or individual employees taking to the roads in cars. Driver fatigue can be an issue when driving any kind of vehicle, such as diggers and bulldozers.

Which is why Caterpillar, in association with Australian company Seeing Machines, rolled out an eye- and face-tracking system that can detect driver fatigue. The system – originally designed for vehicles used in mining but since used in regular trucks – incorporates a camera, GPS and accelerometer. It tracks eye and eyelid movement, such as how often a driver blinks, how long those blinks last, and how slowly the eyelids are moving – and it can do all this even if the driver is wearing sunglasses. It can even analyse the position of the driver's head and whether it has started to drop. When a driver closes their eyes for longer than 1.6 seconds, an alarm is triggered inside the truck – both a noise and a vibration within the seat. Then, if the alarm is triggered for a second time, a dispatcher or supervisor will be contacted, so that they can make contact with the driver via radio. If a third alarm is triggered, the driver would generally be taken off driving duty. The system has been shown to reduce fatigue events by up to 90 per cent.[5] Interestingly, the system can also be used to detect when a driver is distracted and taking their eyes off where they should be – again, triggering an alarm in the cab.

Making industrial and manufacturing settings safer

This vision of a connected worker may soon become standard practice in many industrial and manufacturing settings. Companies such as Honeywell now offer a range of wearable technologies that can improve employee safety. Such devices may gather data on heart rate, breathing, motion, posture and even the presence of toxic gases, with the information pulled together into a dashboard display that gives supervisors and safety professionals an accurate picture of what employees are experiencing in real time.

Of course, most industrial and manufacturing settings involve humans working with machinery – and sensors can also play a vital role in increasing machine safety and efficiency. Sensors can be used to assess machinery compliance, safety anomalies, machine stoppages (and their causes) and much more – all of which helps companies better understand what's going on in real time on the floor and the safety risks, accurately pinpoint machinery misuse and reduce safety-related stoppages. Despite the fact that technology plays a critical role in most industrial and manufacturing settings, safety management has traditionally relied on rather dated methods and information, often based on what's happened in the past or at other locations. The ability to gather real-time insights therefore makes a huge difference.

One way data is proving particularly valuable is in identifying discrepancies between the way machinery and safety systems are designed to be used, and the way they are actually used in practice. For example, data may highlight that emergency stop buttons on machines are not in fact being used in emergencies, but to clear routine jams. This misuse could reduce the efficiency of the safety system and cause it to fail when it's really needed, thus putting people at risk. Insights like this highlight when additional safety training is needed for employees. Plus, with the predictive capabilities of analytics, machine safety systems can predict risk through a detailed risk calculator.

Making construction sites safer

Despite strict safety measures and regulations, construction sites remain some of the most dangerous places to work in the world; in the UK, construction is the third most dangerous industry to work in, and the rate of fatal injuries is around four times higher than the average across all industries.[6] Construction sites are dynamic places, constantly in flux, and each site is different, which makes identifying every possible risk and hazard almost impossible.

However, wearable devices can help construction companies monitor what employees are exposed to and provide safer working environments. Even hardhats are now being made 'smart', and fitted with sensors that detect fatigue in those operating machinery. In another example from the construction industry, sensor data proved that one particular mortar board (those boards with a handle underneath used by bricklayers) actually reduced the risk of bricklayers suffering lower back injury. The EcoSpot mortar board system reduced the amount of time workers spent with their backs bent more than 20 degrees by as much as 85 per cent. Not only that, it led to a 17 per cent increase in productivity (i.e. the number of bricks laid per minute).[7]

Virtual reality and augmented reality are also proving useful safety tools in the construction industry. In site planning, for example, research has shown that VR can help to improve safety by allowing professionals to visualize conditions and identify possible hazards before construction even starts.[8] Crucially, these more immersive tools can simulate actual site conditions in a virtual environment, which makes them more effective than looking at standard two-dimensional drawings. The same research also found that visualization technologies were very effective in immersive construction safety training and education, which makes a lot of sense.

And when construction is underway, AR comes into its own as a safety visualization tool. Naturally, construction workers can't be immersed in VR headsets and blocking out everything around them on-site. Because AR glasses are transparent, the worker stays aware of and engaged with their surroundings, while being fed additional data that's being superimposed over the real world. So, graphics can be overlaid that show where the wiring is, for example. Or, when a worker sees a real-life hazard sign somewhere on the site, AR glasses can display text to explain what the hazard is and what safety measures need to be taken.

Keeping people safe in the heat

Particularly for those who work outdoors or do very physical jobs, extreme heat can present serious risks. Remember the smart hardhats I mentioned? Engineering company Laing O'Rourke, which operates in the Australian outback, has used such technology to keep its employees safe in extreme conditions – smart hardhats fitted with a sweatband sensor that measures the heart rate and temperature of wearers, as well as the external temperature around them.[9] The data is uploaded from the hardhats to the cloud, where it's analysed to look for patterns that suggest a worker might be at risk of heatstroke. If an employee is in danger, the hardhat itself receives a sound and vibration alarm that alerts the worker to take a break in the shade. Such heat sensors could be used in a number of different settings, from fruit farms or vineyards to construction sites.

Looking at the link between connectivity, employee safety and productivity

While it's clear that increased connectivity of both workers and machines can help to dramatically increase safety, it can also significantly boost productivity. Think about the factory machinery example outlined earlier in the chapter – if machinery or safety systems are not being used in the way they're intended, this can lead to earlier failure or extended shutdown for unscheduled maintenance, which obviously impacts productivity. Detailed insights on safety-related issues can improve troubleshooting and resolve downtime issues much faster, and even prevent them from happening in the first place through improved staff training.

The same is true of connected individual workers. We've already seen in this chapter how connectivity helped improve bricklayers' productivity by 17 per cent. Other studies have shown that connected workers are typically around 8 per cent more productive.[10]

The cutting edge of workplace safety: VR and AR

We caught a quick glimpse of how VR and AR can be used to enhance safety on construction sites. But how else are these technologies being used to improve employee safety?

One promising area is the use of VR to provide immersive, highly realistic training simulations for employees. Such training could be used to help workers identify hazards, safely operate machinery and even respond to emergency scenarios (as we saw in the BP example from Chapter 10). In one example, Boeing developed a VR training programme that allows employees to experience certain emergency scenarios, such as a cabin decompression – and the immersive training has reportedly helped the company reduce training time by up to 50 per cent.[11]

But safety training doesn't have to be fully immersive to be effective. AR, which overlays information over whatever the user is seeing in the real world, can also prove very useful in training – by providing employees with safety instructions in real time as they go about their work. The Nsflow platform, for example, works in conjunction with QR scanners, allowing employees to access AR instructions whenever they need them. And if you think VR and AR training only applies to those working in hazardous or highly technical scenarios, think again. Nsflow says its AR training can be applied in all sorts of settings, including offices, clinics, educational institutes and warehouses.

Think of AR training as, essentially, 3D training – a more interactive way of learning safety protocols step by step – and it's easy to see how the technologies could be applied in a wide range of settings. That's the idea behind Vection Technologies' EnWorks AR training solution, which creates three-dimensional training manuals that are designed to replace paper manuals. EnWorks can also be used to create mock-ups of the work environment, allowing employees to practise safety procedures. And when carrying out their jobs, Vection Technologies says EnWorks can provide real-time guidance and reminders, such as identifying potential hazards and displaying instructions.

Circle back to Chapter 10 for more on the use of AR and VR in training.

Improving employee wellbeing and wellness

As well as ensuring working environments are safe, sensors are also commonly used to ensure workplaces are pleasant environments to be in – think temperature sensors, windows that open automatically to control ventilation, and so on. This sort of technology is commonplace in many organizations, so in this section we'll focus on some of the newer ways in which companies are looking after their employees. Much of this focuses on employee health or wellness, and how many organizations are providing data-driven employee wellness programmes.

Why is wellness important?

It makes sense that the healthier employees are and the happier they are, the better they will perform for the company. Some of the most common work-related illnesses include mental health issues (like stress and anxiety) and musculoskeletal problems (such as back pain), and these health issues can cost companies dearly through employee absence and lost productivity.

In this landscape, wellness programmes are becoming more and more popular among employers, in an effort to encourage employees to be healthier – and therefore happier. Such programmes are not just about reducing absence, though; wellness programmes have also been shown to boost employee engagement, performance and retention.[12]

At an individual level, wearable fitness tracking bands such as Fitbit are increasingly being offered to employees either for free or at a subsidized rate in order to help them monitor their activity levels and encourage them to be more active. There's more on this later in the chapter.

And at the organizational level, HR analytics (see Chapter 6) allows employers to analyse data on their wellness programmes – such as data from wearable devices or responses to pulse surveys – to help them better design and manage aspects of employee wellness. For example, if pulse surveys highlight that one aspect of a wellness programme has a take-up that's lower than expected, the company can either modify and improve that part of the programme or replace it with something new.

Looking after your employees' mental health

AI is also playing an increasing role, particularly when it comes to employees' mental health – a good example being the use of pulse surveys and sentiment analysis to identify how employees are feeling. This sort of technology, particularly sentiment analysis, can even pinpoint signs of stress, depression or anxiety in employees.

With 83 per cent of US workers suffering from workplace stress, and one million Americans missing work every day due to stress, this should be an especially big concern for employers.[13] Stress costs companies dearly in terms of absenteeism, lost productivity and employee engagement.

Again, AI analytics of data from pulse surveys can play a huge role in enhancing employees' mental health, by helping you gauge how happy and satisfied your workforce is. Not only can this help to inform your workplace culture, it can also help you design better, more thoughtful wellness programmes.

In one project in Finland, AI is being used to boost employee wellbeing through an app that asks employees questions about their wellbeing. The answers are then anonymized, meaning employers can use the data to create targeted, preventative wellbeing tools – and employees feel comfortable giving honest answers. One employer participating in the project said the tool resulted in employees taking fewer sick days.[14]

As we'll see later in the chapter, AI is even capable of predicting *potential* mental health issues.

Improving physical health with the IoT

As well as identifying when employees are in physical danger, or suffering from stress or anxiety, technology is now able to help employees lead healthier, more active lives. The IoT has played a huge role in this – for example, how many people do you know who wear a fitness tracking band or use an app on their phone to track their activity or number of steps a day? A lot, I bet.

Reducing the risk of back problems

I was shocked to learn that 12.5 per cent of all sick days in the UK are down to back pain.[15] Increasingly, this can be attributed to how many of us sit at a desk all day. We're simply not designed to sit for seven hours a day – even if we do sit correctly with perfect posture the whole time. Most of us struggle to maintain great posture all day – come to think of it, most of us aren't even aware of our posture a lot of the time. Yet poor posture can have serious long-term health effects and shouldn't be overlooked.

While workstation risk assessments and ergonomic products like back supports and footrests go some way to protect employees against back problems, it's clear that more could be done. Part of the solution may lie in IoT. We've already seen many examples of how products and people are becoming increasingly connected – now even your office chair has undergone an IoT makeover. Even with a super fancy ergonomic chair, it's still possible to sit badly because we're generally not aware of our posture while we're busy working away. Now, smart office chairs are being designed with sensors that register the user's posture and make them aware (through vibrations) when they're sitting incorrectly. The idea is that, by increasing awareness of posture throughout the day, employees can modify their posture as needed and avoid back problems in the future.

The role of fitness tracking bands and smart watches

The IoT is also impacting employee health and wellness in more obvious ways: wearable fitness tracking bands and smart watches. These are increasingly becoming part of corporate wellness programmes around the world, including at companies like BP, Bank of America and Target. Fitbit's corporate wellness offering, for example, includes a suite of tools and resources for employers, including dashboards to monitor how employees are doing. And the trackers themselves do far more than encourage staff to get up and walk more; Fitbit claims they also increase engagement in wellness programmes and improve health outcomes. And, particularly in the US, these trackers are also being used to reduce health insurance costs by allowing employers to leverage employee health and activity data to negotiate with insurers.

This isn't to say that you must rush out and buy hundreds of fitness trackers or smart watches for your staff, but it does point to how employees are willing to engage with IoT-enabled wellness programmes. As more and more people are investing in their own fitness tracking bands, and as mobile apps are increasingly offering similar capabilities to track activity and other health metrics, more and more wellness programmes will leverage these developments to their advantage.

Delivering personalized recommendations for employees

As we've seen throughout this book, AI is great for providing personalized recommendations and solutions. Employers are now beginning to use this to deliver recommendations regarding employees' health and wellness. Indeed, AI has the ability to design personalized wellness programmes that are tailored to individual employees – for example, by categorizing employees according to their wellness preferences, and helping people set and achieve their own wellness goals.

This can even extend to recommendations regarding healthcare. In Chapter 5 I briefly mentioned that Walmart has begun using AI to help employees find the right medical provider. How does this work? Walmart has partnered with AI company Health at Scale, which uses AI to give patients personalized recommendations on which provider is likely to provide the best outcomes for them, based on their health needs and medical history.[16] Essentially, the system uses AI to identify healthcare providers who have successfully treated patients with similar needs. Walmart has rolled out the system to workers (and their families) in certain locations, with the tech integrating with Walmart's existing health plan administrator's search engine and virtual care referrals.

The role of predictive analytics in wellness

The next level in AI-enabled employee wellness is using predictive analytics to pre-empt physical and mental health conditions, and help employees get the help they need.

A great example of pre-emptive mental healthcare comes from the AI app Kintsugi, which uses vocal biomarkers to detect signs of depression and anxiety based on just 20 seconds of free-form speech.[17] The app – named for the Japanese artform of repairing broken pieces of ceramic with gold enamel – is language-agnostic, which means it can be used globally, irrespective of the language, dialect or accent. The app aims to offer a diagnosis, where appropriate, plus a treatment plan.

Depending on where you are in the world, accessing mental health services can be a real struggle, so apps like this – offered as part of a corporate wellness offering – could be a lifeline for employees who want to better manage their mental health. That said, there are pitfalls around predicting health issues. More on that coming up…

The cutting edge of wellness: Tapping into VR and the metaverse

I believe we will increasingly see employers use immersive technologies to aid employee wellness. It makes sense when you think about it, since VR can be used to create immersive meditation, mindfulness and relaxation experiences. So why not incorporate this into a wellness offering to help employees reduce stress and feel calmer?

This could prove especially valuable for those working in fast-paced, high-stress jobs. In one study, clinicians working in the UK's National Health Service were offered the chance to participate in a relaxing VR session during the working day. And those who did reported significantly increased feelings of happiness and relaxation. It even helped to lower participants' heart rate.[18]

VR seems a natural fit with wellness. But what about the metaverse? As more and more work activities take place in immersive metaverse environments (like onboarding new employees in the metaverse, see Chapter 8), it's worth considering the potential applications of the metaverse in employee wellness.

In particular, virtual spaces can help employees – especially those who work remotely – feel more connected to their colleagues. And this can have a huge impact on employee satisfaction and happiness. So, in the future, employers might create virtual hangout spaces where employees can gather and share those little 'water cooler' moments. Social events can be held in the metaverse to help foster team spirit. And regular team meetings can be held in immersive virtual spaces, as opposed to a Zoom call. Imagine, for example, gathering your team in a luxurious virtual meeting room with stunning views over a green valley or dramatic mountains. By making everyday aspects of work more immersive, the metaverse may help to enhance employee wellbeing.

The potential downsides of data-driven employee safety and wellness

It's clear that we can monitor increasing amounts of data about employees' activities and health. The question is, how much monitoring is too much? Particularly when it comes to employees' health data, this is obviously highly sensitive and personal data and employers need to tread carefully and act in an open, transparent way (see Chapter 4).

Remember, health data is valuable data

Shockingly, health data is reportedly 10 times more valuable on the black market than credit card data.[19] Large batches of personal health data are especially valuable because they can be used for medical fraud – and because medical fraud is typically slower to detect than, say, banking fraud, it's a far more tempting prospect for criminals than your bank details. Plus, health data is frequently not as well protected as credit card data or other obvious sources of fraud, which makes it an easier target. While this is more of an issue for healthcare providers – who are often operating on old legacy computer systems in desperate need of an update – it still needs to be considered by employers who are working with employee health data. It's imperative you guard this valuable employee data with the same level of protection as you would your customer data.

How much should employers know about their employees?

We know that tracking employee data can have a whiff of Big Brother about it, and sometimes employee scepticism is warranted. One unsavoury report showed how employers were already using data to identify when employees might be pregnant or considering becoming pregnant, before those employees were ready to divulge the news to their employer.[20] Not only is this an invasion of privacy, it also opens up the potential for employers to slyly discriminate against pregnant or soon-to-be-pregnant women (such as overlooking them for promotion) before they've been officially informed of the pregnancy. The argument in favour of such systems is that it can help employers identify when an employee may be at risk of health issues.

But the thing is, employees may not be comfortable with their bosses knowing how fit (or not) they are, or having the ability to identify when they might be at risk of health issues. Back in 2012, Ohio healthcare provider The Cleveland Clinical announced that employees who were overweight or at risk in other ways (such as being a smoker) who didn't join the company wellness programme would have to pay more for their health insurance – over 20 per cent more, in fact. And those that did join the programme but didn't meet health targets set by programme administrators for them also saw their premiums rise by almost 10 per cent.[21] Practices like this are likely to alienate employees and send morale plummeting.

Navigating these challenges

The challenge for HR teams is therefore to encourage participation in wellness programmes and use data to help employees live healthier lives (which, in turn, financially benefits the company) without making employees uncomfortable.

One option is to only use aggregated data, not the ability to drill down to into individual activities. Another is to ensure wellness programmes are voluntary – because, when participation in wellness programmes becomes mandatory, or when employees feel their health data may be used to punish them in some way, buy-in for wellness programmes take a nose-dive. And rather than punishing employees who don't participate – by, for example, putting up their health insurance premiums – it's far better to offer employees lower premiums for taking part. In other words, offering an incentive for employees to take part, but not disadvantaging employees who don't wish to participate.

Finally, we should acknowledge that there are many non-data ways to facilitate employee wellbeing, such as providing on-site exercise facilities or discounted (or free) gym membership, and serving up healthy food in the canteen. Data and AI should never replace good practices like these. But, used well, data and AI can give HR teams precious insights into how to manage and improve employee wellbeing and safety.

Key takeaways

I think employee safety and wellbeing is one of the most exciting and fast-developing areas of data-driven HR. Key points from this chapter are:

- Data- and AI-driven technologies, especially wearable technologies and sensors, are making workplaces safer and more comfortable places to be – from construction sites and factories to regular offices.

- Because IoT devices can transmit real-time data for on-the-fly analysis, managers can be alerted when unsafe practices are taking place and take appropriate action.

- While increased connectivity of both workers and machines can help dramatically increase safety, it can also significantly boost productivity.

- VR and AR also have an important role to play in workplace safety, particularly when it comes to delivering better, more immersive, more engaging safety training – or even step-by-step safety instructions in real time.

- When it comes to wellness, data and AI can play a role in improving employees' mental and physical health – for example, by creating better feedback loops, offering employees wearable fitness trackers, and delivering AI-driven personalized health recommendations.

- VR may also help to enhance your wellness offering, especially in terms of lowering stress.

- It's really important to take proper precautions to protect employee health and wellness data. Also, remember that employees may be uncomfortable with their bosses knowing how fit (or not) they are. The challenge for HR teams is to encourage participation in wellness programmes and use data to help employees live healthier lives without making those employees uncomfortable.

That brings us to the end of Part Two. Now that we've got a good idea of how organizations can use data and AI to deliver more thoughtful, efficient HR services, how can you put these ideas into practice? Turn to Part Three to find out...

Notes

1 D Hardawar. Humans trust this emergency robot more than common sense, Engadget, 29 February 2016. www.engadget.com/2016-02-29-humans-trust-this-emergency-robot-more-than-common-sense.html (archived at https://perma.cc/4CKQ-JW99)

2 Health and Safety Executive. Health and safety statistics: Key figures for Great Britain (2021/2022), Health and Safety Executive. www.hse.gov.uk/statistics (archived at https://perma.cc/NSK5-RXCA)

3 G Schultz. The Holy Grail of safety, EHS Today, 6 February 2014. www.ehstoday.com/safety-leadership/article/21916109/the-holy-grail-of-safety-a-single-allencompassing-safety-leading-indicator (archived at https://perma.cc/L2QY-ZR6X)

4 Science Daily. Electronic nose could aid in rescue missions, Science Daily, 23 July 2014. www.sciencedaily.com/releases/2014/07/140723110403.htm (archived at https://perma.cc/BG8T-ZG8C)

5 L Kelion. Caterpillar backs eye tracker to combat driver fatigue, BBC News, 28 May 2013. www.bbc.com/news/technology-22640279 (archived at https://perma.cc/94ZS-74C9)

6 Health and Safety Executive. Work-related fatal injuries in Great Britain 2022, Health and Safety Executive, 23 November 2022. www.hse.gov.uk/statistics/pdf/fatalinjuries.pdf (archived at https://perma.cc/9F7A-QYX6)

7 S Smith. IOT: Reducing back injuries and costs, improving productivity, EHS Today, 18 April 2016. ehstoday.com/construction/iot-reducing-back-injuries-and-costs-improving-productivity (archived at https://perma.cc/CU7C-RQFE)

8 S Azhar. Role of visualization technologies in safety planning and management at construction jobsites, Procedia Engineering, 2017, 215–26, doi.org/10.1016/j.proeng.2017.01.329 (archived at https://perma.cc/4835-NA6X)

9 A Chanthadavong. Laing O'Rourke monitors workers' safety with a smart hardhat, ZDNet, 17 November 2015. www.zdnet.com/article/laing-orourke-monitors-workers-safety-with-a-smart-hardhat (archived at https://perma.cc/ND5P-NTLZ)

10 Toppan. The role of wearable technology in the workplace, Toppan, nd. toppandigital.com/translation-blog/role-wearable-technology-workplace (archived at https://perma.cc/CX5M-JULK)

11 Ironyun. How AI can improve workplace safety, Ironyun, 20 May 2022. www.ironyun.com/blog/how-ai-can-improve-workplace-safety (archived at https://perma.cc/8RYQ-6S25)

12 S Miller. Wellness programs as an employee retention tool, SHRM, 20 January 2010. www.shrm.org/resourcesandtools/hr-topics/benefits/pages/wellness_employeeretention.aspx (archived at https://perma.cc/4YLR-8YFV)

13 The American Institute of Stress. Workplace stress, The American Institute of Stress, nd. www.stress.org/workplace-stress (archived at https://perma.cc/KT6W-VDDD)

14 European Commission. Using AI to boost productivity – and employee wellbeing, European Commission, European Social Fund Plus, 28 April 2022. ec.europa.eu/european-social-fund-plus/en/projects/ai-boosts-productivity-and-employee-wellbeing (archived at https://perma.cc/CS3B-YHGY)

15 G Wynne-Jones et al. Absence from work and return to work for people with back pain, *Occupational and Environmental Medicine*, 2014, 71, 448–56. oem.bmj.com/content/71/6/448 (archived at https://perma.cc/FCV6-JZ8S)

16 R Torrence. Walmart teams up with Health at Scale to help its workers find the right doctor, Fierce Healthcare, 31 January 2022. www.fiercehealthcare.com/retail/walmart-teams-health-scale-help-its-workers-find-right-provider (archived at https://perma.cc/XXM5-QHEP)

17 A McBride. How AI is transforming employee wellness benefits, VentureBeat, 14 February 2023. venturebeat.com/programming-development/how-ai-is-transforming-employee-wellness-benefits (archived at https://perma.cc/T5R5-2YNC)

18 J S Adhyaru and C Kemp. Virtual reality as a tool to promote wellbeing in the workplace, Digital Health, 4 March 2022. journals.sagepub.com/doi/full/10.1177/20552076221084473 (archived at https://perma.cc/E2RZ-2TRC)

19 N Griffin. Patient data '10–15 times more valuable than credit card data', Irish Examiner, 19 May 2021. www.irishexaminer.com/news/arid-40293149.html (archived at https://perma.cc/7N7J-SDEL)

20 V Zarya. Employers are quietly using big data to track employee pregnancies, Fortune, 17 February 2016. fortune.com/2016/02/17/castlight-pregnancy-data (archived at https://perma.cc/E4AY-RENR)

21 S McGee. How employers tracking your health can cross the line and become Big Brother, *Guardian*, 1 May 2015. www.theguardian.com/lifeandstyle/us-money-blog/2015/may/01/employers-tracking-health-fitbit-apple-watch-big-brother (archived at https://perma.cc/R4NL-ENEQ)

PART THREE
Making data-driven and AI-enabled HR happen

Having explored the various HR services and activities in Part Two – and explored how other organizations are successfully using data and AI – you might be wondering how to apply what you've learned in your own organization. This part will help you on that journey.

Essentially, these chapters answer the question, 'So where do I go from here?' Together we'll look at identifying and prioritizing use cases (key data projects), building the necessary skills and culture for data-driven and AI-enabled success, and creating the right infrastructure. For me, these are the foundations of intelligent HR.

Identifying the   12
use cases for
your organization

Back in Chapter 5, we talked about creating a data and AI strategy. We looked at the importance of linking your strategy to the organization's and HR function's strategic objectives and explored the core questions that form part of any good data/AI strategy. In this chapter we build on that strategic process and look at how to identify specific use cases/projects for your organization.

Why talk about use cases now?

And why not back in Chapter 5, you ask? Well, between Chapter 5 and here, we've explored many ways in which organizations can leverage data and AI – from delivering better HR insights to improving employee safety and wellbeing, and a whole lot in between. Your mind might be buzzing with possibilities. (Great!) Or maybe you feel a little overwhelmed at the thought of applying all that you've learned in your own organization. (Totally understandable.)

As such, now is a good time to press pause and revisit how you can use data and AI *strategically*. How you can best use data and AI to deliver your HR objectives and contribute to the business's wider strategic objectives. Because, yes, there are many possibilities, but they won't all be relevant or realistic for your organization. So how do you know which projects to focus on – and *how many* to focus on? This chapter will help. Therefore, think of this chapter as a bridge between strategy and practical implementation.

Naturally, this is intrinsically linked to the fundamental process of creating a data and AI strategy, so it's a good idea to cast your eye back over Chapter 5 once you've read this chapter (or now, if you prefer).

Identifying potential use cases

In Chapter 5, we briefly looked at the potential ways in which you can use data and AI in HR. Broadly speaking, these fall into three main categories: generating better HR insights to aid decision making across the organization; delivering a better service for employees and candidates; and driving efficiencies in HR.

When identifying potential use cases, these three categories provide a useful jumping off point. I also recommended that you look at your biggest HR and organizational challenges, as these may point to priority projects. And, of course, you'll want to look at the organization's wider corporate objectives to see how you can use data and AI to help deliver the company's mission.

Essentially, you're trying to identify areas where data and AI could really make a difference in your organization – whether that's by solving your biggest challenges, helping to drive the organization forward or simply delivering the best possible HR service.

Start with a brainstorming session

When working directly with clients, I usually recommend starting with a brainstorming session. The size of the session and number of people involved will depend on your organization – it could be one person or it could be everyone in the HR team plus other key stakeholders in the organization.

The goal of the session is to identify specific use cases (or you might prefer to call them 'opportunities') to put data and AI to work. Once you start thinking about it, you'll probably be surprised at how many you can come up with. Don't worry about having too many opportunities on your list. Later on, we'll talk about narrowing your list down. For now, let your imagination loose and try to come up with as many as possible.

That said, it's a good idea to ensure that the opportunities you identify serve at least one of the purposes we've already talked about, i.e. generating better HR insights; delivering a better HR service; driving efficiencies in HR; solving your biggest HR and organizational challenges; and helping the organization achieve its strategic vision. If an opportunity doesn't serve one of these purposes, are you sure it would deliver value for the organization? Remember, just because something *can* be done with data and AI, doesn't mean it *should* be done.

Quick wins and transformational projects

Next, I recommend organizing your list of opportunities into two categories:

- The first category is 'quick wins' – projects that provide immediate returns for a relatively low investment. Quick-win projects are great because they help you hone data and AI skills, build confidence in using these technologies and ultimately create buy-in for bigger initiatives. Speaking of which...

- The second category is 'majorly transformational' or 'strategic, longer-term' projects – those game-changing applications of data and AI that may require a bigger upfront investment and longer development period, but which can create a fundamental change in the way HR serves the organization (or even a fundamental change for the organization itself).

Narrowing down your priorities

You've found where the opportunities lie and categorized them according to quick wins vs. transformational projects. Now you need identify your top priorities.

The truth is, some of the ideas you've come up with during brainstorming are likely to be completely unrealistic, or too technical, expensive or difficult to do right now, and that's fine. Up until now, the exercise has been focused on identifying opportunities and, by doing so, understanding how and where data and AI could be useful. That in itself is a valuable process. But since you have to be realistic, you'll need to create a shortlist of your top priorities – the use cases which are most viable to put into operation and will deliver the most value.

In my experience, the teams and organizations that are most successful at leveraging data and AI tend to be those that start out with a small but highly focused number of use cases – use cases that all closely align with strategic goals. If you pick too many, it can quickly become unmanageable due to the number of variables and the large number of stakeholders involved. Particularly within organizations where there is perhaps not widespread buy-in for digital transformation, attempting too many use cases at once can lead to overwhelm, disappointment and an ongoing lack of engagement (the old 'I knew it was a waste of time, and I was right' attitude).

Another danger of attempting too many initiatives all at the same time is that it can be difficult to determine exactly what is affecting what! You can easily get to the point where one initiative is impacting metrics associated with another initiative, and you might not know whether change is happening for the reasons you expect, or whether it's happening because of something completely unrelated.

Clearly, you need a shortlist. But how many opportunities should make it onto that list? Generally, I think it's a good idea to prioritize between one and three 'major' use cases, depending on the size of your organization and budget, and one to three 'quick wins'. It's important to have a spread across both categories – meaning you need the 'quick wins' to help build trust in what you're doing, and you need the more majorly transformational use cases to demonstrate long-term value.

Fleshing out your use cases

For each use case that you've prioritized, you'll now want to answer the following questions. (By the way, I have a handy 'use case template' with all these questions on my website, bernardmarr.com – and it's free to download.) Apply this list of questions (or fill out the template) for *every* use case you've prioritized.

The questions are:

1 **How does this use case link to a strategic goal?** Because intelligent HR is all about using data and AI to solve problems, reach your goals and help drive the organization forward.

2 **What is the objective of this use case?** Back in Chapter 5 we talked about identifying your most pressing unanswered business questions – those questions you need to answer if you're to achieve your strategic goals. You'll probably find that answering those questions will be the objective of your chosen use cases (or be very closely linked to the objective).

3 **How will you measure the success of the use case?** There's not much point doing anything with data and AI if you can't tell whether you've been successful or not. This means you will have to define what success looks like, and identify the indicators that you can use to measure success.

4 **Who will be the use case owner?** Every use case needs someone who will take overall responsibility for ensuring that it can be delivered. Someone who's responsible for making sure it is planned and implemented at a tactical level. Of course, particularly in a smaller organization, there may not be enough people involved for every use case to have a different owner, so one person might take responsibility for several use cases.

5 **Who will be the data customers?** These are the people that will monitor and act on the insights discovered by the use case. They could be HR personnel, or people in other business functions (department managers, for example). It's important to understand who these people are to ensure that the use case and resulting insights can be communicated in a way that will be actionable by the people that matter – the data customers.

6 **What data do we need?** At this point, you need to think about where you will get the information needed to answer the key business questions and achieve the use case objective. You may find that you already have (or can get access to) all the information you need within the organization itself. On the other hand, you might identify knowledge gaps that need to be filled by looking outside of the organization to external data sources.

7 **What data governance issues need to be addressed?** As we've seen throughout this book, data and AI are hugely powerful tools for driving business change, but they also bring important challenges around governance, compliance and regulation (Chapter 4). A wrong step here can have serious repercussions – and not only in a legal sense. Privacy, consent and data bias will be key considerations here.

8 **How do we analyse the data and turn it into insights?** Once the data has been collected, you need to turn it into insights. For that, you need to choose the right analytics techniques (text analytics, for example).

9 **What are the technology requirements?** Here, you start to identify the specific technology infrastructure requirements (more on this coming up in Chapter 14). For 'quick win' use cases, particularly in smaller organizations with limited budgets, a cloud-based HR analytics platform may well deliver everything you want. For larger projects, you may need a more specialist solution.

10 **What skills and capabilities do we need?** Next, you have to assess the human skills and resources needed to get the job done. (This is the subject of Chapter 13.) You may or may not have these capabilities in house. If not, you have three main options – upskill the existing workforce, hire new people with the skills you need or outsource the project to external partners and service providers.

11 What are the issues around implementation we need to be aware of?
The final point to consider at this stage is what practical considerations might prevent you moving your use case from idea, to plan, to execution? In particular, you'll want to make sure there are clear lines of communication between all involved parties, but specifically between the people whose job it is to pull out the insights, and the people whose job it is to take action on them.

Linking your use cases to your wider data/ AI strategy

Some of the above questions will be familiar because they featured in Chapter 5. In other words, Chapter 5 helps you focus in on your overarching objectives/challenges/unanswered questions, but many of the same strategic questions also apply to each individual use case.

If you haven't yet created your overarching data and AI strategy, that's fine. Because you can in fact use your fleshed-out use cases to form the framework of your strategy. After all, each priority use case aligns with an HR goal or challenge – and your strategy is all about delivering your goals and solving your problems. What's more, by fleshing out your use cases, you've gained an understanding of data requirements, infrastructure implications, and so on – and you'll probably find, having been through the process of fleshing out your use cases, that there is some crossover between the use cases in terms of data, skills required, governance issues, etc. There will be synergies and potential efficiencies that could feed into your strategy as a whole. This is particularly true with governance considerations, as these will typically apply across all of your use cases.

And if you *have* already created an initial data and AI strategy, now is a great time to revisit it, with your priority use cases in mind. This is the perfect opportunity to look at how your use cases affect your strategy as a whole. And how your strategy as a whole ties in with your use cases.

Now is also a good time to think about budgeting. If one of your use cases is likely to eat through a large portion of your budget, you might struggle to get everything done. For this reason, you should think about budgeting for your priority use cases as a group, rather than as individual projects.

Learning from other businesses that have been on the data and AI journey

Let's revisit a couple of examples from this book and re-examine them from a use case perspective.

The huge multinational

I referenced Shell in Chapter 3 and talked about how the company's GameChanger unit partnered with video game start-up Knack to identify the key characteristics of top idea generators within the business. Let's pretend we were in the room when Shell first identified this data opportunity. In this case, the underlying objective was to help the company more easily identify the best ideas among those submitted to the GameChanger unit – thus ensuring that great ideas don't get overlooked and that those working in the GameChanger unit can focus their time and attention on ideas that are likely to deliver the best value. You could say their unanswered questions here were, 'What characteristics unite our best idea generators?' and 'How can we assess people for those characteristics?' The strategic link is crystal clear.

Just as an aside, I've worked with Shell on their AI strategy, and it's important to note that, even though Shell is a large organization with impressive resources, we still limited ourselves to no more than three transformational use case priorities, plus a couple of quick wins. Because even large companies (some would say *especially* large companies) run the risk of getting caught up in the excitement of data and AI, and losing sight of what they're trying to achieve. So it goes to show that if a huge organization like Shell can drill down to a handful of priority use cases, you can too.

How a tech trailblazer got it wrong

Amazon has placed data and AI at the very core of everything it does: intelligent products (such as Alexa and Echo), intelligent services (for example, Amazon's personalized customer recommendations) and intelligent business operations (such as warehouse operations that are highly driven by data).

Yet, in Chapter 4, we saw how Amazon had to stop using a machine learning algorithm that was designed to assess job applicants, after discovering that it was, well, sexist. No doubt this use case started with the best strategic intentions – to save recruiters time, to provide a more efficient HR service to candidates and perhaps even (ironically) to reduce the risk of human bias in the recruiting process. But, clearly, where this use case fell short is in the governance and implementation considerations. When fleshing out this potential AI opportunity, did the possibility of data bias come up for discussion? When looking at the potential implementation pitfalls, what mechanisms were considered to ensure the algorithm was fit for purpose before being rolled out? Were the measures of success perhaps flawed, in that they focused more on efficiency as opposed to the quality and diversity of candidates?

We can't answer those questions for certain. But it goes to show that even extremely tech-savvy businesses have had to navigate the process of becoming an AI-enabled, data-driven organization – and they don't always get it right. We can all learn from this, by which I mean pay close attention to the governance issues, measures of success and potential implementation roadblocks.

This use case aside, one thing that really impresses me about Amazon is how seamlessly different divisions have got behind data and AI – from the ecommerce side of things, to its AI-as-a-service offerings, to the fulfilment operations. Building a culture of data and AI is crucial to success in intelligent HR. But more on that coming up in the next chapter…

Key takeaways

To summarize the key points on identifying use cases in your organization:

- When it comes to identifying potential data and AI opportunities, start with a simple brainstorming session. The goal of the session is to identify specific ways (or opportunities) to put data and AI to work.

- Next, categorize your use cases according to quick wins and major transformational projects. You need a mixture of both, because quick wins help to build trust and demonstrate the value of data and AI (in a relatively quick and inexpensive way), while the transformational projects bring huge value for the long term.

- Now it's time to identify your top-priority projects – as in, those that are most viable and/or deliver the most value. It's a good idea to prioritize between one and three major use cases, depending on the size of your organization and budget, and one to three quick wins.

- If you haven't yet created your overarching data and AI strategy, your use cases can form the framework of that wider strategy. And if you have already created your data and AI strategy, now is a great time to revisit it, with your use cases in mind. After all, there will be issues and considerations that are common across all use cases.

Whatever your use cases, a lack of data and AI skills can be a major barrier to implementation, especially in smaller organizations. So let's explore this topic of skills and competencies. In the next chapter we'll see how HR teams can prepare themselves for the intelligence revolution, overcome the data skills shortage and build a culture of data and AI.

Building skills and aligning culture 13

Back in Chapter 10 we talked about essential future skills for the workforce – emphasizing soft skills just as much as (if not more than) technical or digital skills. But since this journey of data-driven and AI-enabled HR obviously requires certain data and AI skills, let's dwell a little on that topic. How can you build (or tap into) the right technical skills for intelligent HR – especially bearing in mind the huge global shortage of digital skills? And how can you create a culture that understands the value of data and AI? We'll explore those questions in this chapter.

But first, as an HR professional, what sorts of skills do you personally need to succeed? Let's find out.

What skills do HR professionals need?

The same 20 future skills from Chapter 10 clearly apply to HR professionals as much as the wider workforce. But, specifically for HR roles, I believe the following skills and characteristics are absolutely vital for success:

1 **Communication** – HR professionals must be good communicators, especially in this era of rapid transformation, rising automation and continual education. It's vital you can communicate well with others so that you can both support people through change and avoid misunderstandings. And we mustn't forget that listening is a core communication skill that will serve any HR professional well.

2 **Empathy** – The ability to put yourself in someone's shoes is essential for providing an excellent HR service, and helping the organization manage change successfully.

3 **Discretion** – HR professionals routinely deal with sensitive, highly personal information, and encounter difficult situations (such as harassment). This requires the ability to be discreet, to communicate carefully and sensitively and to keep confidential information private.

4 **Ethics** – Similar to discretion, in that behaving ethically means keeping sensitive information private, and so on. But, more than that, modern HR requires you to have a good understanding of ethics and ethical challenges – especially around the changing nature of work, the role of new technologies in the workplace and being able to harness data and AI without alienating employees.

5 **Organizational skills** – Now more than ever, there's a lot of information and responsibility flying around the average HR role. From keeping track of evolving regulations and compliance issues, to helping the workforce cope with change – not to mention providing an awesome day-to-day HR service – today's HR professionals have to be organized and skilled multi-taskers.

6 **Problem solving** – Aside from the major challenges that digital transformation brings to the workplace, HR teams face perennial challenges such dealing with employee conflicts, or how to identify and attract the best talent. Excellent problem-solving skills are therefore a must.

7 **Decision making** – Oh boy, do HR professionals have to make some tough decisions! Decisions that can affect people's lives in major ways. Despite this, you must be comfortable grappling with difficult decisions and finding the best solutions. As we've seen throughout this book, data can play a huge role in improving decision making. Which brings us to…

8 **Data literacy** – Intelligent HR means working with data on a daily basis. Using data to inform decisions, drive HR efficiencies and provide a better HR service. It's therefore really important that all HR professionals are comfortable working with data (and keeping data safe). But let me add a caveat here – because being data literate should not come at the expense of the more human 'soft' skills like communication and empathy.

In other words, being an effective HR professional in this era of rapid transformation requires a blend of digital and soft skills. And that's true regardless of your specialism within the HR field. Even if your role is heavily focused on HR analytics, for example, you still need to be an excellent communicator, empathetic, and so on. Or let's say you specialize in training and development – you still need to be data literate.

Data literacy and HR

Since data underpins everything about intelligent HR, let's delve into this notion of being *data literate*.

What does data literacy look like, and why does it matter in an HR context?

In essence, data literacy is the ability to understand, work with and make sense of data. It includes the ability to think critically about what the data is highlighting, to ask questions about where the data comes from and how reliable it is (considering potential bias, and so on). And, perhaps most importantly of all, it includes the ability to apply data in your work and turn insights from data into action – be that through your own decision making or by communicating the data to other decision makers in the business.

A data-literate HR professional understands that data is one of the most precious assets an organization has. And that data can add serious value for the organization. In today's highly digital world – where almost everything we do can be measured – this ability to work with data is more important than ever. Because, as we've seen throughout this book, data can lead to better decisions (i.e. decisions that are based on hard evidence as opposed to gut instinct or what's worked in the past), deliver new efficiencies in HR (using HR chatbots, for instance), and help to enhance HR services (such as better recruitment, or learning and development).

How can HR teams develop data literacy?

The first step is to be open to working with data. Don't be afraid of data, basically. Even if you're not a typical 'numbers person', embrace the idea that data can enhance the work that you do.

It's well worth investing in data literacy training – either training that's developed specifically for your organization or the HR function, or more general data literacy training that's offered by any of the major learning platforms. (I give some tips on data courses later in the chapter.)

If you already have an HR analytics tool, get stuck in and experiment with it. Get familiar with using the tool, interrogating the data, and creating outputs (visualizations, reports, etc.). If you don't yet have an HR analytics tool, you can polish up your Excel skills – although an HR analytics platform will obviously help you work with data in more advanced, and often more intuitive, ways. Thanks to these new analytics tools, it's becoming much easier to interrogate data – so you don't need to be a statistician or data scientist to work effectively with data.

You should also start using data as the basis of team discussions. In HR meetings ask questions such as 'What does the data say about this?' or 'What evidence do we have to support that?' Making data a part of everyday discussions in this way ensures the whole HR team views data as a key business asset.

Working with internal data experts

If your organization has a central data team or analytics function in house, connect with them and ask them for the support you need. Indeed, involving in-house specialists, if you have them, is a vital part of creating your data/AI strategy and fleshing out your use cases (see Chapters 5 and 12). But you can also connect with your in-house experts in less formal ways, for example by inviting them to talk about their work at an HR team meeting, or just asking them questions about their work.

Wherever possible, I think it's really important have a central data or analytics group within the organization – people whose job it is to immerse themselves in the data, but work closely with other teams to support their needs. (This is often referred to as the 'hub and spoke' model in data terms, where the central data team is the hub responsible for the organization's data platforms and tools, while the spokes are the various business functions, each of whom have their own data and data needs.) In large HR teams you may even want to recruit your own data scientist or data group that sits within the HR function.

That said, I recognize it's not possible for every organization to have a central data team, or for HR functions to have their own data specialist – and we'll talk more about that later in the chapter. In such cases, it's especially important that you work to improve data literacy among everyone in the HR team and the organization as a whole. I'm not talking about becoming data scientists yourselves. Rather, I'm talking about being comfortable working with data and using data in your everyday work.

Raising data literacy across the organization

HR must also play a vital role in raising data literacy in the wider workforce. This starts with establishing current levels of data literacy in the organization – for example, are teams and individuals routinely using data to back up their decisions? Knowing where the organization is right now gives you an idea of where people may need to boost their data literacy skills.

It's also really important to communicate why data literacy is essential for your organization's success. As with any new initiative, when people understand the 'why', they're more likely to support it.

Of course, it's likely that employees will need some training on the importance of data and how to use the data. Again, this can be a purpose-built training solution for your organization, or you can tap into one of the many courses already on the market. As part of this, teams must be taught how to think critically about data. Just as in the HR team, every employee should know to ask questions such as 'How was this data collected?', 'What can be learned from this data?' and 'How reliable is this data?' Employees must also be trained on the safe and ethical handling of data.

And, naturally, people must also have *access* to the data they need to do their jobs. It sounds obvious, I know, but too often I see teams that simply can't access the information they need on a daily basis. While this is beyond the scope of the HR team, it's an important point to raise. What you don't want is a situation where employees have to rely on data experts to manipulate data for them. Simple self-service tools (like your HR analytics tools) are the best way forward.

Addressing the data skills shortage

We can't ignore the fact that, around the world, demand for data and other technology skills massively outstrips supply. So what does this mean for your ability to tap into data skills?

Hiring in a skills shortage

Demand for work involving advanced data analytics and AI is growing every day and there just aren't enough people with data and AI skills to go around. As an example, the number of job openings posted on sites like LinkedIn and Glassdoor for people with data science skills is growing exponentially and, according to data gathered by Quanthub, the number of posts exceeds the number of people searching for these jobs by a factor of three.[1] And what talent there is tends to be hoovered up by giants like Google,

Apple, Microsoft, IBM, and so on. For everyone else, attracting the right talent is a real challenge.

Naturally, this may impact your ability to hire people with data and AI skills. Which means you may need to get creative. One option is to recruit people who have strong analytical skills, as opposed to specific data science or AI skills – mathematicians, for example, or people with a background in statistics. You can then train them to use the required data and AI tools.

As with any position, the ability and desire to grow is incredibly valuable. Someone who doesn't tick all the boxes on paper but is very keen to learn new skills and grow with the business will always be a better fit than someone who is fixed in their ways and unwilling to learn – no matter how experienced and knowledgeable they are in data and AI. Besides, the world of analytics and AI is moving so fast and new technologies and applications are emerging all the time, which means the ability to adapt and learn is becoming increasingly important.

Upskilling existing employees

If you don't have a central data or analytics team, and hiring in-house expertise isn't an option, how else can you tap into data skills? The first option is to upskill your existing employees. Not just in terms of data literacy – which is a must for all employees – but also in terms of more advanced AI and data science skills.

The truth is, while you want everyone in the organization to become more confident around data and future technologies, it's likely that 'star players' will start to emerge across the business – people who have a natural affinity for working with data and AI, even if they don't necessarily have formal training in them. Investing in more advanced training and upskilling for these team members is likely to bring the greatest rewards. You might even start thinking of these people as your 'data ambassadors' – people who can spread the word about data and how it benefits the business.

Upskilling a workforce can take some time but it doesn't necessarily have to be hugely expensive. Lots of free and inexpensive training material is available online, from both universities and organizations. Some resources to consider include:

- 'A crash course in data science' by John Hopkins University, which is available on the Coursera online learning platform
- 'Introduction to data science', available for free on Alison.com

- Various data science courses available on datacamp.com
- 'What is data science?' by IBM – another course available through the Coursera platform
- 'Google data analytics professional certificate' – going a little deeper than some of the above introductory courses, this course aims to set anyone up as a professional data scientist in six months. While it's primarily aimed at those seeking a first job in data science, the skills taught are equally valuable for someone looking to upskill within their own organization. You can find this course on Coursera.

Tapping into skills outside the organization

When upskilling employees isn't an option, or you need more immediate support, you'll have to start looking outside the organization for skills and capabilities.

Your main options here are:

- outsourcing to an external provider
- acquihiring
- setting up a tech incubator/innovation hub
- crowdsourcing

Outsourcing to external providers

There is a large market of providers out there who can handle your data and analytic needs – and the market is growing all the time. Whether you're looking for an all-in-one service covering everything from collecting data to presenting key insights, or you just need some help with applying AI analytics to data that you already have, there will certainly be a provider who can meet your needs.

Generally speaking, you can partner with a provider for the longer term – or, if you don't want to be locked in with a specific provider, you can outsource on a project-by-project basis. Personally, I tend to favour more of a partnership approach rather than straight-up outsourcing, as that way your partner is likely to be more invested in achieving your organization's goals and vision. Partnering may also help you boost skills within your organization – aiding knowledge transfer, as opposed to simply offloading your projects onto another firm's to-do list.

Some of the biggest data and AI providers are household names like Facebook, Amazon and IBM, and they all offer consultancy services and practical tools, but you certainly aren't limited to the big corporations. There are plenty of smaller contractors out there and these may provide a more personalized, tailored service or have specialist knowledge of your industry. In fact, in my experience, industry-specific providers are becoming the norm as opposed to big generalists.

When looking for a third-party provider, it's a good idea to start with recommendations from your networks and contacts. Failing that, there are many case studies available online and in books (including my own books *Big Data in Practice: How 45 successful companies used big data analytics to deliver extraordinary results*, and *Artificial Intelligence in Practice: How 50 successful companies used AI and machine learning to solve problems*) and these help to highlight providers who are doing excellent, innovative work.

It's vital you partner with a provider who understands what you're trying to achieve. The better your contractor understands your key business questions, your strategic goals and the challenges you face as you work towards those goals, the more likely they are to get to the insights you really need. Always ask for examples of their other client work – even if you've read about their work in case studies or they came recommended to you by a trusted contact. You will want to find out as much as possible about how their previous projects unfolded, what the key challenges were and, crucially, what *concrete results* the clients saw as a direct result of working with that provider. Also consider whether specialized knowledge of your business sector is important or not, as that will inform the selection process.

Acquihiring

Acquihiring (a mash-up of 'acquisition' and 'hiring') is proving a popular solution for many businesses. The term refers to the emerging trend where companies who need to boost their AI and data skills simply acquire small start-ups. By buying up a small start-up, the acquirer gets quick access to data engineers and scientists who have experience building and training AI models – thereby accelerating their progress.

However, as with any acquisition, there are pitfalls to this approach. One MIT study found that a whopping 33 per cent of acquihired talent leave in the first year after purchase,[2] which demonstrates the importance of managing the transition carefully and looking for acquisitions that are a good cultural fit with your own organization.

Setting up a tech incubator or innovation hub

Another way to access external skills is to set up a tech 'incubator' or innovation hub, which can be a good way for companies outside the tech industry to gain access to talent and foster collaborations with AI experts. For example, brewer AB InBev – the world's largest brewer, and makers of Budweiser, Stella Artois and Corona – has created a Silicon Valley innovation hub called the 'Beer Garage' to explore how cutting-edge technologies like AI can help drive performance. The Beer Garage is designed to help the company research, develop and test technology-driven solutions – but also puts the company in close proximity to the vast network of tech companies and venture capitalists in the Silicon Valley area. This fosters collaboration with local start-ups and helps to drive innovation. The company says it's learning a lot from working with these inspiring tech experts.[3]

Crowdsourcing

One final option that may be worth considering is crowdsourcing platforms such as Kaggle – a competition-based platform that allows businesses to tap into an army of armchair and citizen data scientists. As we saw in Chapter 7, even large corporations like Walmart have turned to Kaggle to find analytics talent.

Kaggle acts as a middleman: companies bring their data (whatever it may be), set a problem to solve as well as a deadline and offer a prize (usually cash, or sometimes a job). It's a fascinating idea which has so far seen contestants compete to solve problems ranging from analysing medical records to predict which patients are likely to need hospitalization, to scanning the deep cosmos for traces of dark matter. Hal Varian, Chief Economist at Google – another mega-company that has used Kaggle's services – has described Kaggle as 'a way to organize the brainpower of the world's most talented data scientists and make it accessible to organizations of every size'.

When working with a crowdsourcing platform, you might want to use synthetic data, to avoid privacy concerns or any worries about commercially sensitive data falling into the hands of competitors via a public platform.

Crowdsourcing has great potential for identifying emerging talent and it provides businesses with new ways of engaging with people who can potentially help them solve their problems and answer key business questions. And because the competitive element ensures those taking part will strive to make sure their ideas stand out from others, this encourages out-of-the-box thinking that can lead to some very innovative solutions for businesses. So, if you are struggling to attract talent or, for whatever reason, you don't want to partner with an external provider, crowdsourcing your data analysis could be an option. It's a great way to supplement skills, access additional analytical brainpower and test the waters on new data projects.

So which approach is right for your organization – crowdsourcing, acqui-hiring, setting up a tech incubator or partnering with third-party providers? It's likely you'll need a combination of these different strategies rather than relying on one single approach.

And remember, for relatively simple data and AI projects, many off-the-shelf HR analytics tools can meet your needs and require little or no prior knowledge to get started. They're designed for HR professionals, after all, not data scientists.

Preparing for a cultural shift in HR and the organization

It's virtually impossible to realize this vision of intelligent, data-driven, AI-enabled HR if the HR team – and indeed, the organization as a whole – isn't on board with data and AI initiatives. You therefore need a culture that recognizes the importance of data and AI. A culture of innovation that embraces change and continual learning. A culture that's open to new opportunities instead of clinging stubbornly onto old ways of doing things.

Technology has always brought about new ways of working, but what's different about the current wave of transformation is the sheer pace of change. AI in particular is going to fundamentally change the work that humans do. And not in a generation's time – I predict we'll see enormous changes within the next five to ten years. The HR team and the organization as a whole must start to prepare people for these changes and build a culture that embraces rather than fears change.

Seeing automation as a positive force

I don't want to downplay the impact of automation – in many industries and jobs, the impact of automation will be keenly felt, and many jobs will change or be displaced. However, it's really important to recognize the positive side of automation and AI. Because, just as the previous industrial revolutions have ultimately *created* more jobs (and better jobs), AI and automation will create more jobs than are destroyed. My hope is it'll create *better* jobs for humans.

In fact, AI has been described as 'the greatest job engine the world has ever seen'.[4] Rather like the internet before it. Yes, the internet had a negative impact on some jobs, but look how many more jobs it's created and how it's enabled businesses to branch into new markets, reach new customers, streamline their business processes, and so on.

Research by Capgemini backs up this idea of AI and automation augmenting rather than displacing human workers altogether. In a survey of 1,000 organizations that have already deployed AI-based systems, four out of five companies had created more jobs.[5] I spoke to one of the survey respondents, insurance giant Prudential. The company's global head of AI, Michael Natusch told me, 'Instead of looking for ways to replace humans with AI, we are seeking the most fruitful complements.'[6] He cites robotic call centre assistants as one example. 'Clearly, nobody wants to talk to a robot. But if a robot answers a phone call on the second ring and provides the right information at the right moment in time, then there is value in this. Our call centre agents appreciate the collaboration with robots as they are now able to focus on harder problems that require their experience, creativity, and empathy.'

In other words, AI systems are great at automating the boring, mundane and repetitive stuff, those tasks that are easily repeatable, rules-based and uncreative. And this, in turn, allows humans to focus on more creative, empathetic and interpersonal work.

All this means it's important to approach automation and AI with an open mindset – and for the organization to find ways to *augment* the work of human employees, rather than making it redundant altogether. It's about using AI to help people do their jobs more efficiently and add greater value to the organization.

HR's role is to guide the organization through this process, to help find the right balance between machines and humans, and, of course, prepare people within the organization for change. Whatever changes take place in your organization, it's important that people feel change is not *done* to them. That they have opportunities to learn and enhance the work that they do.

What this means for human skills

When parts of jobs are automated by machines, that frees up humans for work that is generally more creative and people-oriented, requiring skills such as problem solving, empathy, listening, communication, interpretation and collaboration. These are the skills we looked at in Chapter 10 – skills that humans are still better at than machines.

According to Deloitte, as machines take on the mundane, repetitive work, jobs become more human, which makes the work and contribution of people in the workplace more valuable and important. This is borne out by the results of a Deloitte global human capital trends survey:[7]

- 62 per cent of respondents were using automation to eliminate transactional work and replace repetitive tasks.
- 47 per cent were using automation to improve existing work practices and boost productivity.
- And 36 per cent were 'redesigning work' as a result of automation.

The upshot is that individuals and organizations will need to develop both the technical (data literacy and tech awareness) and softer human skills to succeed. Employees at most levels will be required to access data and work out what action to take based on what the data tells them. And everyone must be able to understand the potential impact of new technologies on their industry, company and job. And, on top of that, most employees will need to cultivate softer skills like communication and creative thinking.

This is why it's so important to foster a culture that embraces continual learning and curiosity.

Building an AI and data culture – practical steps

To recap what we've covered so far in the chapter, if you were to create a roadmap of how to build the right culture for data-driven and AI-enabled success, it might look something like this:

Step 1: Redefine work and the role of people

What does work look like in the HR function and the wider organization in future? Much of today's work is geared around performing a particular function. But this is likely to change as organizational structures become more fluid. The focus will shift to projects and outcomes rather than particular tasks that need to be repeated over and over again (because the latter is exactly the sort of work that machines excel at). People within the HR team and the wider organization will need to develop the skills and mindset to cope with this, but they can't do it alone – HR needs to lead in this area, to show how data and AI can add serious value for the organization.

Step 2: Improve technical skills

As I've said, we won't all need to be data scientists or AI experts in the future, but we will *all* need some degree of data literacy. The HR team and wider organization will need to develop data literacy skills so that people are equipped to take advantage of AI and data, and learn to ask questions such as 'How can we use this to improve performance?', 'How can we ensure we're using this technology ethically?' and 'How accurate is the data we're working with?' Most likely, you will also need to beef up the company's more advanced technical capabilities, whether that means partnering with external providers, acquihiring, crowdsourcing or hiring in-house data and AI experts.

Step 3: Develop human potential

As machines begin to master more tasks typically performed by humans, humans must begin to focus on the areas in which they outperform machines – creativity, imagination, critical thinking, communication, and so on. As such, your learning and development programmes can't afford to overlook these inherent human abilities.

Step 4: Redefine learning to focus on continual learning cycles

One report by Dell Technologies and the Institute for the Future predicts that 85 per cent of the jobs that will be available in 2030 don't exist yet.[8] People will no longer start a career path and grow with one role, and many of us may be doing very different jobs in a decade's time. Which makes learning all the more important. But not just learning; continual learning. As the world of work continues to evolve, education, learning and training must become a continual endeavour.

How to successfully manage change

We know that change can be painful, and badly managed change can sap morale, reduce performance and ultimately hinder the adoption of new practices or technologies. It's therefore up to the HR team to carefully manage change.

Communication is key here. When people don't understand why change is happening, they're much more likely to resist it. Demonstrating the clear link between AI and data initiatives and the organization's key strategic priorities helps to secure buy-in, as does showcasing success stories. (You can always showcase examples from other companies that have successfully harnessed data and AI, perhaps using some of the examples from this book.)

This is also where your 'quick win' use cases come into play (see Chapter 12), since these help you demonstrate the value of data and AI, in a relatively short space of time and for relatively little spend.

What's more, it will be up to HR teams to listen to employees' concerns and provide reassurance. Many people assume AI and automation will lead to job losses, but that's not necessarily the case. AI will create more jobs than it displaces. And even for those jobs that are impacted by automation, the likelihood is that many of them will change rather than be lost altogether. Engaging and involving everyone in these discussions is key for getting people on board with change.

Key takeaways

To summarize the key takeaways from this chapter:

- It's vital that everyone in the HR teams sees data as a key asset, and that HR professionals build their own data literacy. It's also up to HR to lead the way in developing data literacy across the wider organization.

- When it comes to tapping into data and analytics skills, the ideal options are to work with your organization's central data/analytics team, or maybe even hire data/AI specialists into the HR team. Recognizing that hiring won't be an option for many businesses – especially given the current shortage of available tech talent – other options include upskilling the existing workforce, partnering with third-party providers, acquihiring, setting up a tech incubator or crowdsourcing your data analytics needs.

- It's vital organizations and individuals prepare for the changes that are coming our way. This means building data skills and capabilities, but also developing our uniquely human soft skills.

- You want to build a culture that embraces data, AI and automation. But to do this, the HR function needs to listen to the workforce and ensure people do not feel like change is being *done to* them. Those companies that can build a positive data and AI culture, successfully manage change and bring everyone along on this transformative journey, are the ones that will succeed.

Of course, skills and culture aren't the only ingredients for data-driven and AI-enabled success. You also need to build the right technology infrastructure. In the next chapter, we'll explore the different layers of technology infrastructure that you will need to consider.

Notes

1   Quanthub. The data scientist shortage in 2020, Qaunthub, 2020. quanthub. com/data-scientist-shortage-2020 (archived at https://perma.cc/D7SD-4ZXL)

2   M Somers. Your acquired hires are leaving. Here's why, MIT Sloan School, 8 January 2019. mitsloan.mit.edu/ideas-made-to-matter/your-acquired-hires-are-leaving-heres-why (archived at https://perma.cc/KLX2-BABW)

3   B Marr. The amazing ways the brewers of Budweiser are using artificial intelligence to transform the beer industry, Forbes, 9 September 2019. www. forbes.com/sites/bernardmarr/2019/09/09/the-amazing-ways-the-brewers-of-budweiser-are-using-artificial-intelligence-to-transform-the-beer-industry (archived at https://perma.cc/UK8F-S43R)

4   B Reese. AI will create millions more jobs than it will destroy. Here's how, SingularityHub, 1 January 2019. singularityhub.com/2019/01/01/ai-will-create-millions-more-jobs-than-it-will-destroy-heres-how/amp (archived at https://perma.cc/2RJQ-FHRZ)

5   Capgemini. Artificial intelligence – where and how to invest, Capgemini, nd. www.capgemini.com/service/digital-services/insights-data/data-science-analytics/artificial-intelligence-where-and-how-to-invest (archived at https://perma.cc/P6NV-XMQV)

6   B Marr. Instead of destroying jobs artificial intelligence (AI) is creating new jobs in 4 out of 5 companies, Bernard Marr, nd. bernardmarr.com/default.asp?contentID=1194 (archived at https://perma.cc/N5GH-ME64)

7   J Schwartz et al. From jobs to superjobs: 2019 global human capital trends, Deloitte, 11 April 2019. www2.deloitte.com/us/en/insights/focus/human-capital-trends/2019/impact-of-ai-turning-jobs-into-superjobs.html (archived at https://perma.cc/TH7K-RFNS)

8 Dell Technologies and Institute for the Future. *The Next Era of Human–Machine Partnerships*, Dell Technologies and Institute for the Future, 2017. www.delltechnologies.com/content/dam/delltechnologies/assets/perspectives/2030/pdf/SR1940_IFTFforDellTechnologies_Human-Machine_070517_readerhigh-res.pdf (archived at https://perma.cc/V4NP-9K94)

Creating the technology and data infrastructure

14

By this point in the journey, you've created your data and AI strategy, identified your use cases and considered the skills and capabilities that you need. Now's the time to think about technology. You might be surprised that technology comes so late in the process, but that's deliberate. You should never start with the technology itself, because that's a sure-fire route to 'technology for technology's sake'. But with all your requirements fleshed out, you can finally begin to identify the technology – i.e. the software and hardware – that will help you deliver your goals.

But first you need to ensure that the HR tech/IT strategy fits with the organization's wider technology strategy and infrastructure. So that's where we'll start this chapter. After that, we'll move onto the infrastructure itself, and explore the three layers that you need to consider before investing in any technology.

Your HR technology strategy – and how it fits with the wider business strategy

It's really important to align any HR technology infrastructure with the overall technology infrastructure in place in the organization. What I mean by that is, the vendors that you use and analytics products that you choose might be informed by vendors and products that the organization already deploys elsewhere in the business. (Of course, they might not, if there really is no relevant infrastructure already in place in the organization. My point is, you should look at existing frameworks before bringing new technology or vendors into the organization.)

Obviously, this is something you'll want to discuss with your IT team (and central data team, if there is one). No doubt your business will have a wider technology/IT strategy in place that covers the business as a whole, so that's a good place to start your discussions.

You may also have your own HR technology strategy (that covers the wider HR tech landscape, not just data and AI). If that's the case, you should review that strategy in light of your data and AI requirements. And, in the process, ensure your HR tech strategy is aligned with the business's overarching tech strategy.

If you don't have an HR technology strategy, we'll look at that next. But again, you'll want your HR technology strategy to be an extension of the entire organization's technology strategy.

The key point, then, is to ensure there's a clear line of sight between your HR technology strategy, and the wider business technology strategy – just as you would ensure a clear line of sight between the HR function's strategic goals and the organization's strategic goals.

What is the HR technology strategy? (And is it different from your data/AI strategy?)

The HR technology/IT strategy is like a roadmap that sets out how the HR function can get the most out of technology and transform HR workflows. In other words, it looks at the broader digitization of the HR function, not just the role of data and AI (although, naturally, the data and AI component will form a major part of your technology strategy). So, it might cover HR social media usage, for example, or job application systems, as well as people analytics systems.

Creating a technology strategy generally involves:

- Confirming the HR function's strategic goals. Because your technology strategy should cascade down from HR goals, which in turn cascade down from the wider business goals.

- Looking at the HR technology already in place, and assessing whether it's fit for your current and future needs. Basically, are your technology systems supporting your goals?

- Assessing existing technology tools and providers – again, to ensure they meet current and future requirements.

- Identifying technology infrastructure gaps and skills gaps that need to be filled in order to deliver the HR function's strategic goals.
- And, of course, identifying your strategic data and AI requirements, as we've discussed elsewhere in this book.

Ordinarily, this would all be developed in partnership with your IT function. Your IT colleagues will be able to advise on technology solutions and providers, and work with you on implementation – but it's up to you, the HR function, to maintain a laser-like focus on your strategic goals. To put it another way, your IT colleagues are the technology experts, but you are the expert on exactly what it is that HR is trying to achieve.

As we saw in Chapter 13, it's not just about having the right strategy in place, or inspiring use cases in mind – you also need to create the right culture and foster the skills that will help you execute your strategy successfully. So do circle back to Chapter 13 for a recap on skills and culture.

Ensuring your technology strategy stays agile

As with any strategy, it's really important that your technology roadmap can flex and adapt to changing needs. Because, as we've seen throughout the book, things are changing fast. You need your technology systems – data- and AI-related systems and other systems – to be able to respond to change without causing major upheaval.

As such, I recommend reviewing your HR technology strategy on an annual basis to assess how you're doing against your plan and where things have changed (both in terms of HR requirements and the wider business direction).

When it comes to the technology itself, the wide array of cloud-based 'as-a-service' solutions typically provide plenty of 'plug and play' options – meaning you can quickly reconfigure your subscription, turn on new options and turn off services that you no longer need. Staying agile is therefore easier than it used to be, back when investing in new software and hardware meant a big financial outlay and long-term commitments. That said, do keep the need for agility in mind as you assess technology options. Always try to choose technology solutions that are flexible, and can scale up or down according to your needs.

Putting in place the right data and AI infrastructure

Now, finally, we come to the process of identifying the right data- and AI-related technology for you. In essence, this is where you decide on the software or hardware that will take your data and turn it into insights. It's likely you will need to invest in some tools and services to make this happen, even if your company already has some existing data/AI infrastructure in place. And the good news is, you have more choice than ever.

Until recently, it was difficult for the average business function to work with a wide variety and volume of data without making heavy infrastructure investments – expensive software and hardware, storage facilities, a team of data analysts, and so on. Thankfully, that's no longer the case. Developments like data- and AI-as-a-service and the ever-expanding market of third-party providers now allow even the smallest company to harness data and AI relatively easily.

When thinking about the technology infrastructure you need, there are three layers to consider:

- infrastructure to collect data
- infrastructure to store data
- infrastructure to access and analyse data

We'll discuss each layer below. But, given that most companies have some existing infrastructure in place, it makes sense to consider what you already have in relation to each of these layers. Therefore, as you work through these sections, make a note of what technologies your organization already has in place (work with your IT or data team on this). You will probably have to make changes and additions to existing infrastructure, but just keep in mind that some of your existing systems may have a role to play in meeting your data and AI needs. For example, you might already be collecting useful data through your customer service centre, even though you don't yet have the ability to analyse it. Depending on your use cases, you might want to consider whether your existing infrastructure could be updated to give you those abilities.

Ultimately, there's no one-size-fits-all solution. Believe me, it would be great if I could just say 'any HR team should buy this infrastructure-as-a-service solution from company X' but in reality, you are going to have to work through each of the following layers and consider what will be the best fit for each of your data and AI use cases. Again, you should work with your IT/central data team as you consider each layer. And if you don't have in-house expertise to help you assess infrastructure needs, remember that there are plenty of data and AI experts out there – myself included – who can consult with you.

Layer 1: Infrastructure to collect data

The data collection layer is where the data arrives at your company, whether it is internal or external data, structured or unstructured. This may include data from your employee feedback, recruitment channels, social media channels, sensors (either wearable sensors or on machines) or any other source. Match the data that you have available to the data requirements of your chosen use cases and see if there are any holes that need filling.

You might need to source some or all of the data required, and sourcing new data might mean it's necessary to make new infrastructure investments.

If your requirements are for external data, then it's just a case of finding the right provider, and you might not need to make any infrastructure changes at all. Often, 'off the shelf' cloud services can simply be plugged into freely available public datasets and set to work. But if you're looking for more specialized data, such as data on your specific industry, then it's likely you will need to find an appropriate data broker. Luckily, as businesses have reaped the benefits of moving to data-driven decisioning, a market has sprung up where data on just about any industry or activity is up for sale, for those who need it.

If your requirements are for internal data, you will have to find the infrastructure tools you need to collect it. Circle back to Chapter 3 for a reminder of the different types of data available these days (such as sensor data, activity data and conversation data) – and how to collect it. Remember that synthetic data may be a good option when the data you want doesn't exist.

Exactly what tools or systems you need for capturing data will depend on the type of data you need, but some options include:

- sensors
  - fitted to devices, machines, buildings, vehicles, packaging, employee badges or anything else you want to capture data from
- CCTV and video
- website cookies

- employee feedback systems
- employee communication systems
- social media feeds

Be aware that collecting new forms of data introduces new vulnerabilities to your organization, and you'll need to take the necessary steps to protect that data. But we'll talk more about that in the next layer…

Layer 2: Infrastructure to store data

Having identified your data capture needs, next you have to think about where you will keep your data. The main choices we have here are between traditional, on-premises data warehouses and cloud-based systems. Often, though, this won't be an either/or decision, as hybrid options are becoming increasingly common.

On-site storage options

As far as on-premise storage solutions go, regular hard disks of very high capacity are available very cheaply these days, by enterprise IT standards. If you're a small business and you don't need to store a huge amount of information for frequent, high-volume analytics, this might be all you need.

Other options include solid state storage solutions, and even old-fashioned magnetic tape. Solid storage is most frequently used for smaller volumes of data that you need to access very frequently, as they offer very high access speeds but are relatively costly. The price of this storage is falling all the time though, and in the future it's likely to become an increasingly viable solution for large-volume, long-term storage. Compared to mechanical, magnetic hard disks, solid state drives offer very high reliability, low failure rates and low latency, which makes them ideal for tasks where speed and precision are key.

Magnetic tape solutions may seem old-fashioned and often people that I speak to are surprised to find that they are still a viable commercial option in this day and age, but in fact a 2019 survey found that 90 per cent of the organizations surveyed still rely on tape data for some of their storage requirements – often a considerable amount.[1] Tape storage is mainly used because it is very cheap in comparison to other storage media, so for data that needs to be archived long-term and accessed very infrequently, it's often the ideal choice.

In the cloud

These days, however, there are many reasons that you might choose to forego on-premise data storage infrastructure, or at least complement it with off-premise solutions, in the form of cloud storage solutions.

Just as is the case with cloud-based analytics solutions, cloud storage solutions offer the advantage of letting you get up and running right away. What's more, cloud storage is incredibly flexible, you can create additional storage whenever it's needed and when you take up-front set-up costs into account, it's generally the more affordable option – particularly if you're planning on scaling up to work with bigger and bigger datasets.

Cloud storage simply means that your data is stored on servers that are owned and operated by a cloud service provider, usually remotely, but connected to the internet so you can access the data from anywhere at any time. There is a high amount of built-in redundancy, meaning that your data is distributed as multiple copies in numerous locations, so if one cloud data centre experiences problems, you will still be able to access your data. The price will change according to how much data you store or the volume of data you stream in and out of the cloud.

With cloud, security is certainly an important consideration. It might seem logical to assume that storing data outside of private company servers inevitably creates risk, and it does. However often this is offset by the overall robustness of the security provided by global enterprises that have built their entire business model on data. You can (hopefully) be relatively confident, for example, that a large cloud provider will keep all of its software patched and up to date. Firewalls will be in place to prevent DDOS attacks and the physical premises where the data is actually stored will be patrolled by security guards. Additionally, as mentioned above, your data is likely to be spread and duplicated across multiple locations, so even a catastrophic event like a fire or earthquake hopefully won't result in the loss of all of your data. Of course, it's possible to make sure all of these measures are in place when you are storing all of your data on-premise, but it's a big responsibility.

The difference between public, private and hybrid cloud

Public cloud generally refers to cloud services provided by a third-party organization that specializes in doing so. The data itself is not usually public – rather, 'public' refers to the fact that the third-party organization provides cloud computing services to customers (either individuals or businesses) and anyone can use them. The biggest public cloud providers at the moment are:

- Amazon Web Services
- Microsoft Azure
- Google Cloud Services
- Alibaba Cloud
- IBM

Private cloud, on the other hand, is simply a term for what companies do today when they maintain everything in-house, but following similar models of deployment, access management and infrastructure maintenance as the public cloud providers. A company that outsources all of its data and computing requirements to another organization – one that does not also offer the same services publicly – could also be considered to be operating a private cloud infrastructure. The primary reason for doing this is often security – in some cases, businesses will be working with data that is so sensitive that it isn't permissioned for storage outside of the organization's immediate jurisdiction. Additionally, your own private cloud infrastructure can be configured exactly as you require.

Of course, as with everything related to analytics and even computing in general, with cloud there's no one-size-fits all approach. This has led to the emergence of what are termed 'hybrid-cloud' and 'multi-cloud' models.

Hybrid cloud usually refers to a solution comprised of elements of public and private clouds. This can be useful when, for example, a subset of the data you are using is too sensitive to let out of your hands, but other data is safe to host publicly, where you can take advantage of the infrastructure that public providers make available. This creates a very agile environment where the best elements of each ecosystem are on-hand, as and when they are needed. A challenge is that software needs to be able to communicate across public and private servers, even if it can't access the same data on each one, but this is generally catered for by the big providers of hybrid cloud services.

Another option that you might come across is known as *virtual private cloud*. This is usually a service offered by a public cloud provider that will deploy its infrastructure within your own premises or data centre, again with the aim of creating a 'best of both worlds' situation, where you have the total control of everything being under your roof, while also benefitting from the tools, services and interfaces provided by the public provider.

Finally, *multi-cloud* refers to picking and choosing different solutions from different cloud providers. Sometimes this is to ensure the highest level of availability, particularly if you are serving data to users or customers spread throughout the world.

The importance of avoiding data silos

An essential factor when deciding where to store your data is accessibility. This doesn't just mean making sure you can get hold of it when you need it – it means making sure it's as readily available as possible to those who need it throughout the organization. These decision makers may not be part of the HR function, but they may still need access to HR data in order to make better decisions and drive performance. This thinking goes as far back as 2002 when then Amazon CEO Jeff Bezos issued a 'mandate' that all data was to be made as widely available throughout the company as possible.

Siloing is something that occurs in organizations when data is collected by disparate teams and simply stored without any consideration for whether it might be useful for another team. Often, one team doesn't even know what data the other team has, and over the years this can lead to countless wasted hours and money as data capture and storage is replicated. Basically, data silos happen because, in the average business, data lives in multiple systems and locations across the company, with each team only having access to 'their' data, and having no idea what other data might be available elsewhere in the business. As you can imagine, this reduces transparency and collaboration – the very opposite of what you want to achieve with intelligent HR.

So how can you spot a data silo? Dead giveaways are when data is inconsistent or conflicting across the business, or when data is hard to access. Another is when department heads or managers complain that they simply don't have the data they need to do their job.

Data silos are a major problem for the organization as a whole to address – ideally by investing in infrastructure that allows data to be stored in one easily accessible place. Even when data comes from multiple sources, it can still be stored in one place. The organization should also have company-wide procedures in place for managing and maintaining data.

This isn't to say you shouldn't have your own HR data systems. Naturally you will. But it's really important to consider the need to share data with others in the business, and ensure data is easily accessible to those who need it. This is also why it's so important to align your strategy with the wider business technology strategy. By aligning the HR strategy with the organization's overarching technology strategy – and by considering who else might need access to your data – you should be able to avoid the data silo trap.

Keeping your data safe

Data security is another key consideration that falls under data storage. It's vital that you take steps to keep your data safe from accidental loss or malicious data breach. Both of these can have legal ramifications under legislation (such as GDPR), but are also essential considerations of any data governance policy.

The heaviest governance burdens lie with personal data. However, one of the most useful ways to reduce your liabilities is to follow a strategy of data minimization. You can also take steps to anonymize personal data, severing the link between the data itself and the person related to that data.

Data breaches are an increasingly prevalent threat to business. But, again, there are some steps you can take to mitigate these risks. One is a system of permissioning that defines who is allowed access to any particular set of data. Another is the use of encryption – because if data is encrypted it's far less useful to anyone who might want to steal it. You might want to consider homomorphic encryption as an option. Here, data is encrypted in such a way that it can be analysed while remaining in its encrypted form – even the analytical algorithms don't 'see' the unencrypted data. The data can even be edited in the cloud by people with the right permissions, without the unencrypted data being exposed to the cloud servers.

Two other techniques that can be used to de-identify data are masking and tokenization. Masking involves obfuscating sensitive elements of the unencrypted data with other data of the same type, while leaving other elements intact. This might involve swapping, say, all of the information in each 'city' field for a different city. Only those with the correct permissioning will see the correct data, but the data still remains useful for many applications. Tokenization is similar but replaces key or sensitive parts of the dataset with anonymized, randomized tokens. Unlike with encryption, there's no mathematical way to reverse-engineer the original data from the hidden data (which is possible with huge amounts of computing power with many forms of encryption). This is because the tokens are randomly assigned rather than being mathematically derived from the original data. Also, while encryption is typically applied to a whole record, tokenization (and masking) are generally applied to specific fields within the record.

Circle back to Chapter 4 for a recap on the major data and AI risks, and how to overcome them. But, overall, it's important to remember that data security is a highly specialized field and it's something you will probably want to discuss with experts.

Don't overlook threats from the IoT

The ever-increasing number of smart, connected devices has led to a rise in the angles of attack that hackers have at their fingertips. According to research, millions of IoT devices have security vulnerabilities that can be exploited to allow unauthorized access to data.[2] From machine sensors to smart employee badges, think of every connected device you have in your network as a 'door' into your company – a door that has to be kept locked and secure from intruders, just like any other door.

A very important practical first step is to ensure you always change any default passwords or login information – this is often the way that many IoT devices are compromised. This is also another area where a policy of 'minimization' can pay dividends. Consider just how connected you need your equipment to be – of course, most devices need to interface with a smartphone or computer app, but do they really need to be able to connect and interface with any other devices? Be sure to understand exactly 'what is talking to what'.

Layer 3: Infrastructure to access and analyse data

Finally, you need to consider how you will process and analyse the data you've collected and stored, in order to extract the insights you need. In Chapter 3 we looked at the main options currently used for data analytics, many of them falling under the heading of AI. This layer is about selecting the tools (i.e. analytics software) that you need to do this.

The process of extracting insights from data can be distilled into three steps:

1 preparing the data – identifying, cleaning and formatting it so it can be analysed efficiently
2 building the analytics model
3 drawing a conclusion from the result of the analytics

As with storage functions (layer 2), much of this data processing layer is now done in the cloud (although some of the analytics providers can deploy cloud on-premise – depending on the decisions made during the previous layer). Options like BigQuery (Google), Amazon Web Services and Microsoft

Azure HDInsights all provide tools that carry out analytics on whatever data you throw into them. In addition, Amazon QuickSight, Infobright, IBM Cognos Analytics, Hortonworks Data Platform, Cloudera Data Warehouse, Pivotal Analytics, Sisense, Alteryx, Splunk and SAP Analytics Cloud are all tools that have proven their capabilities and are used by businesses globally. As well as these established companies, a large number of start-ups have emerged offering solutions tailored to specific workloads or industries.

This layer is really where AI comes into its own, because many of the advanced analytics options on the market are built on machine learning. But before you invest in infrastructure or an 'off the shelf' AI analytics service, do remember to look at the systems already in place in the organization. In other words, while there are plenty of HR-specific analytics tools on offer, you want to make sure your chosen option fits with the business's wider strategy. For example, if your organization is already using a certain analytics platform, first consider whether that platform has an HR offering.

You will also want to consider how you'll communicate insights from the data to the people who need them – within both the HR team and other decision makers in the business. Ultimately, this is about putting systems or processes in place to make sure insights are easily accessible and understandable.

Key takeaways

Here's what we've learned about infrastructure requirements:

- It's vital you ensure there's a clear line of sight between your HR technology strategy and the wider business technology strategy – just as you would align HR's strategic goals with the organization's overarching strategic goals.

- The HR technology/IT strategy is like a roadmap that sets out how the HR function can get the most out of technology. In other words, it looks at the broader digitization of the HR function, not just the role of data and AI (although, naturally, data and AI will form a major part of your technology strategy).

- While you will work with IT on developing (and implementing) any HR technology roadmap, during that process your role is to remain laser-focused on HR's strategic goals. (So, HR takes the lead on what it wants, and IT helps to achieve that.)

- When it comes to putting in place the right infrastructure, there are three layers to consider: infrastructure to collect data; infrastructure to store (and protect) data; and infrastructure to access and analyse data.
- Given that most companies have some existing tech infrastructure in place, it makes sense to consider what you already have in relation to each of these layers. So, for each layer, do consider what technologies your organization already has in place. You might have to make changes and additions to existing infrastructure, but just keep in mind that some of your existing systems may have a role to play in meeting your data and AI needs.

We've come to the end of our data-driven and AI-enabled journey. So let's conclude with a look ahead to the future, and see what's in store for intelligent HR over the next few years.

Notes

1 K D Schwartz. Tape storage is 'still here', IT Pro Today, 7 February 2019. www.itprotoday.com/backup/tape-storage-still-here (archived at https://perma.cc/UR52-BF4H)

2 D Palmer. These new vulnerabilities put millions of IoT devices at risk, so patch now, ZDNet, 12 April 2021. www.zdnet.com/article/these-new-vulnerabilities-millions-of-iot-devives-at-risk-so-patch-now (archived at https://perma.cc/J3N6-RE67)

The future of HR 15

The work of HR has been utterly transformed over the last 10 years by data and, more recently, artificial intelligence. I hope this book has inspired you to embrace this wave of transformation. To use technology to deliver better people-related insights, provide a more thoughtful, personalized HR service and to harness emerging technologies to make HR even more efficient.

Future trends that will shape HR

If you think HR (indeed, the wider workplace) has changed a lot in the last 10 years, you ain't seen nothing yet. The next 10 years will see yet more transformation, both for HR and for business as a whole – and this transformation will be driven by AI, digitization and automation. As such, the HR functions of the future are likely to be radically different as we see new technologies emerge. And as the technology evolves, so too will society. As a result, what we regard as 'workplace norms' will also evolve. I'm writing this in 2023, and I can already see that work will look very different in 2033 than it does today.

So I thought it would be fun to close out the book with a few predictions for the future of work (and, in turn, intelligent HR). I believe some of the biggest trends to prepare for are:

- radically altered job roles
- decentralized and total-remote work structures
- fully integrated AI systems
- demand for holistic employee experiences

Let's explore each one in turn.

Radically altered job roles

In the future, my school-age children are likely to do jobs that don't yet exist. Jobs I can't even imagine. If that sounds far-fetched, cast your mind back to when you were at school – perhaps jobs like blockchain developer, podcaster, machine learning engineer and social media influencer didn't exist then. (They certainly didn't exist when I was at school.)

Advances in technology, especially automation, will alter job roles drastically. New jobs will emerge, some jobs will disappear (but more will be created in their place) and many jobs will be altered to some degree.

Make no mistake, this is just as true for HR professionals as it is for the wider organization. The work that you do within the HR function may look quite different in 10 years' time. Naturally, the underlying goals and values will be similar (to serve employees, to help your organization succeed, and so on). But your day-to-day activities? They will likely evolve over the next decade.

Because even those jobs that aren't displaced by automation will use data and AI tools to get the job done more efficiently. Marketers, for example, will be able to generate rich (written and visual) content at the touch of a button. Security guards will be able to analyse masses of security footage for suspicious activity, in real time. Designers will be able to use generative design software to create hundreds of potential designs based on their specifications, within the space of a few minutes.

This is already happening, of course. But the transformation will accelerate over the next decade. HR will need to manage this transition – both in terms of the HR team itself, and preparing the organization for the future of work. Reskilling and upskilling will be a critical part of this.

Decentralized and fully remote work structures

As technology continues to evolve, there will be increased opportunities to work remotely in a more seamless way – collaborating and sharing with colleagues as if you're in the same room. Consider advances such as Meta's Horizon Workrooms – a metaverse co-working space where anyone can come and work. More employers will have virtual offices where employees can gather (perhaps using VR) for co-working or immersive meetings.

We may even see more companies become fully remote, with teams distributed across the globe and no one central 'head office'. Why not? With a global talent pool and the technology to make remote collaboration smoother, why should employers choose one spot to set up home? Which means HR will need to be prepared to manage teams that might never meet in person.

Plus, as organizations become more decentralized, the role of HR might shift from managing 'regular' employees in a traditional corporate hierarchy, to managing networks and ecosystems comprising traditional employees, freelancers, contractors – and, of course, bots and AI systems. The word 'team' may mean something rather different in the future. Something altogether more fluid, porous and dynamic than the static, traditional teams that we've grown used to.

These are interesting and exciting prospects. But there will certainly be challenges in terms of team building, maintaining the right culture and keeping employees happy and engaged. The HR teams of the future will need to come up with novel approaches to solving these challenges – and, as usual, technology will have a role to play in that.

Fully integrated AI systems

Increasingly, AI will be ubiquitous across the organization. Including the HR function. In other words, we can expect AI to be fully integrated into the very fabric of HR. From recruiting and onboarding talent, to managing performance, training people and delivering an awesome employee experience, AI systems will be involved at every step of the employee lifecycle.

I'm particularly excited about AI's potential to deliver a more personalized, predictive HR service. For example, algorithms could provide highly tailored career development paths for each employee – something that would be extremely time-consuming and ambitious for human HR professionals to complete (in a large organization, at least).

Bottom line, in the future, you probably won't even have to think about AI – it'll be there, underpinning everything you do, in one way or another. It will be utterly enmeshed with the work of HR.

Demand for holistic employee experiences

No doubt you've noticed employee expectations evolve over the last decade. People – especially (but not exclusively) younger workers – increasingly expect their employer to be diverse and inclusive, to provide flexible working opportunities, and to treat them as individuals rather than just cogs in the machine. They expect to feel connected to the organization's wider purpose and values. They want to feel enriched by their work. And I'm not talking about cool gimmicks like nap pods or grow-your-own-veg beds in the car park. Employees want to feel like the work they do *matters*. That they're contributing to something genuinely valuable.

As employee expectations continue to evolve over the next decade, employees may demand a more holistic work experience that balances their personal and professional lives. HR will therefore need to build frameworks that support this balance. As such, the importance of employee wellness programmes will likely continue to grow. And with advancements in healthcare technology and wearable devices, HR could provide highly personalized wellness programmes that track both physical and mental health – potentially even integrating genomic data to provide personalized health plans.

Ultimately, technology has a big role to play in providing a holistic employee experience. But we can't ignore the fact that technology also has the potential to take the shine off an otherwise positive employee experience. If people don't have the right technology tools to do their job properly, for instance, that will sap morale. Or if they aren't trained properly in new systems. Or if they worry that an algorithm will take their job (concerns that may be unfounded), and that they won't have a chance to upskill and transition to new work.

So while technology can help HR teams provide a more holistic employee experience that helps people balance their personal and professional lives, it's also important to get the basics right. To ensure people can get the best out of technology in their job role so they can truly enjoy the awesome employee experience that you're creating.

Building the workplaces we want

These future trends are obviously driven by technology, but one thing I really want you to take away from this book is that we need to keep humans at the centre of everything the HR team – and the organization as a whole – does. It's vital you maintain a tight focus on the people in your organization, and how you can use data and AI to better serve them.

You have an incredible opportunity before you. An opportunity to use data and AI to add value and create the workplace that you want. Dare I say, it's not just an opportunity, it's an obligation. I write a lot about future technologies and I'm always keen to press the point that we should be using technology to tackle the world's biggest challenges and build a future that we want to live in. Work plays a massive part in that. And so, too, does HR. It's up to HR functions to harness data and AI to make their organization *a better place to work*.

It's no small task, I know. And I understand that widespread transformation – which is, after all, what we're facing – can be incredibly daunting. To counter any sense of overwhelm, I ask you to cast your mind back to the last massive wave of transformation, when computerization began to transform workplaces in the late 20th century. Computers made work and life easier, created value-adding new jobs, and ultimately made the world a smaller, more connected place. (If your memory doesn't stretch back that far, you can take my word for it.)

Has it been a perfect journey? Of course not. Was that wave of transformation wholeheartedly embraced by everyone at the time? Absolutely not. But did the rise of computerization ultimately lead to better, easier lives for most people? I believe the answer is yes.

I therefore believe this coming wave of transformation will make the world better. Despite the many challenges that come with technology – especially AI and automation – I do believe it will continue to make work and life better for most people. In particular, it has the potential to free up the human workforce to focus our time and talents where they matter most. And that goes for HR, too.

Tell me what you think

Now we've come to the end of our journey together, I'd love to hear what you think about the future of intelligent HR. Much as I love writing books like this, it's even more important for me to establish a dialogue beyond these pages. So feel free to ask questions or share your thoughts. Tell me, how is your workplace being transformed by new technologies? Where do you see the biggest challenges and opportunities for HR going forward? How do you envision the workplaces of the future taking shape? How do you see your own job role evolving?

And, of course, you can always get in touch if you need help planning for and implementing data-driven, AI-enhanced HR in your organization. I consult with businesses of all shapes and sizes.

You can connect with me on the following platforms:

LinkedIn: Bernard Marr

Twitter: @bernardmarr

YouTube: Bernard Marr

Instagram: @bernardmarr

Facebook: facebook.com/BernardWMarr

Or head to my website at bernardmarr.com for more content (including my podcast), and to join my weekly newsletter, in which I share the very latest information.

INDEX